A PRICE GUIDE
to
ANTIQUE
TOOLS

A PRICE GUIDE
to
ANTIQUE TOOLS

Third Edition

Herbert P. Kean

THE ASTRAGAL PRESS
Mendham, New Jersey

Published by

The Astragal Press

P.O. Box 239

Mendham, NJ 07945-0239

First Edition: Copyright 1992 by Herbert P. Kean & Emil S. Pollak

Second Edition: Copyright 1998 by Herbert P. Kean

Third Edition: Copyright 2001 by Herbert P. Kean

Cover photo by Robert Garay

Book design by Martyl J. Pollak

Cover design by Donald Kahn

Manufactured in the United States of America

Library of Congress Catalog Card Number 00-112130

ISBN 1-879335-97-2

Third Edition

TABLE OF CONTENTS

INTRODUCTION

"Be judicious in your use of price guides. No price guide can begin to cover the tremendous variety of tools that are available, or accurately reflect the wide diversity in price because of variation in condition of the tools. And in a field developing as rapidly as antique tools, price guides can easily go out of date. Guides do provide information that can be helpful, but you should appreciate their limitations."

–from *Collecting Antique Tools*

Coverage

Rather than attempting to cover *all* antique tools (a somewhat impossible task), the emphasis has been put on those tools that are available, affordable, have visual appeal and historic interest. A few top-of-the-line "specials" have been noted on occasion, just to spice the reader's appetite. **Unless otherwise stated, the most common model of any particular tool has been selected for pricing**. Where applicable, the reader is referred to the Bibliography for more detailed information concerning the rarer models.

Condition

The condition categories and definitions currently being used in the tool world have been followed. The Condition Chart which appears on pages 4 and 5 defines the seven categories that most tool collectors use: NEW (N), FINE (F), GOOD PLUS (G+), GOOD (G), GOOD MINUS (G-), FAIR (Fr), and POOR (P). This chart is based upon the one that originated with Vern Ward in the *Fine Tool Journal* of 1983. Condition greatly affects price, but it is a very subjective process. To help refine the process, additional descriptions are given in each chapter, preceding the tools being discussed.

Prices and Price Range

Tools are bought and sold in a variety of marketplaces, from tailgating at tool club meetings to flea markets, garage sales, antique shows, dealer shops, and auctions (both live and on the Internet). The prices in this *Guide* are based mainly upon the results of over 15 tool auctions conducted during 1999 and 2000 — from small country-style to large international auctions and Internet auctions. Auction prices were predominantly used, as they could be easily and authentically documented from the Prices Realized lists published by the auction houses. They are a strong central basis.

These prices have been transformed into a **price range** for each tool . The range shown covers the condition categories GOOD and GOOD PLUS. A price range is used rather than

1

a single price to allow for the normal variations that occur within any condition group. It also takes into consideration such things as size. In establishing the boundaries of the range, isolated instances of abnormally high or low prices have been omitted.

Other Variables Affecting Price

1. *The extent of the accessories included with the tool*, e.g., extra plane irons, brace pads, etc. These, as well as the price adders for each, will be mentioned where applicable.

2. *Whether the tool is in its original box*. This applies mostly to Stanley and similar tools. In recent years, the presence of the original box has often doubled (or more) the value of the tool. Exceptions will be pointed out.

3. *Maker*. Unless otherwise stated, unsigned tools will be used as the basis for pricing. Signed tools will almost always sell at higher prices than unsigned ones, and signed tools will generally sell for higher prices in the geographic area in which they originated.

4. *Type of material used,* e.g., species of wood or kinds of metal. Where pertinent, differentiations will be made.

5. *Current Trends*. Aside from the effect of the Internet auction, which has brought many new collectors into the field, antique tools have shown two major trends in the past few years:

• Signature pieces have become more interesting (and consequently more sought-after) and their values have grown comparatively greater than unsigned pieces. This is expected when a collectible reaches the "mature stage."

• Large pieces, especially if they are in the primitive category, have lost favor to the more aesthetic, smaller pieces that can be easily displayed.

Condition Chart

The range that is shown for each tool covers the area of condition that we are most likely to find in our normal hunt. Conversions are listed below for the two categories above the range (FINE and NEW), and the category just below the range (GOOD MINUS). No conversions are shown for FAIR or POOR, as tools in these conditions are generally used for parts only, or to show an extremely rare example.

To adjust prices for a condition other than the range shown (bottom of GOOD to the very top of GOOD PLUS), the following conversions are suggested:

NEW or UNUSED (near mint): Add 50% to 100% to the top of the range shown. The amount of the adder is based upon how frequently the particular tool is found new.

FINE: Add up to 50% to the top of the range shown. (Rarer models could go up to a 100% adder.)

GOOD MINUS: Subtract 25% to 50% from the bottom of the range shown.

Remember that condition ratings will most likely vary from one collector to another. Be prepared to see some ratings differing from your own by as much as a full category. This can easily happen when disclaimers are added to the description, e.g., "Missing a cutter and wedge, otherwise FINE." This could be an accurate **physical** description, but unless you re-rate it according to the chart on the following pages, you might price it incorrectly! It would be more correct, **for pricing purposes,** to call this example GOOD MINUS. What you really want to know is its MARKET VALUE AS-IS. And the Condition Chart will do that for you.

Summary

The reader will find this *Guide* most helpful in pricing antique tools. However, *condition is a key factor in price.* Merely looking up a tool in the index and taking its price from the appropriate page will rarely give a complete picture. Its condition must be checked against the Condition Chart *and* the special variables set forth at the beginning of each tool category.

The Condition Chart is shown on the next two pages.

CONDITION CHART - Part I

Based upon

THE FINE TOOL JOURNAL CONDITION CLASSIFICATION
FOR ANTIQUE TOOLS

CATEGORY	USEABLE	FINISH	WEAR	REPAIRED or MISSING
NEW or UNUSED (N)	Totally	Metal - 100% Wood - as mfg'd.	None	None
FINE (F)	Totally	Metal - 90-100% Wood - 80% original or old finish.	Very light	None
GOOD + (G+)	Yes-may need minor tuning.	Metal - 75-90% Wood - well-patinated appearance.	Light	Repair very minor and correct.
GOOD (G)	Yes-may need serious tuning.	Metal - 50-75% Wood - pleasing patination; some stains.	Moderate	Repair minor and correct.
GOOD – (G-)	Probably	Metal - 30-50% Wood - some patination; prominent stain or discoloration.	Heavy	Repair major and correct, or minor and improper. Missing minor parts.
FAIR (Fr)	Probably not	Metal - 0-30% Wood - extreme stain or discoloration.	Excessive	Repair major and improper. Missing major parts.
POOR (P)	No	Near unrecognizable.	Totally worn out	Beyond restoration.

CONDITION CHART - Part II

Based upon

THE FINE TOOL JOURNAL CONDITION CLASSIFICATION
FOR ANTIQUE TOOLS

	REPLACED PARTS	SURFACE	MISCELLANEOUS
N	None	Metal - no rust. Wood - surface smooth, edges sharp.	OB= Original Box. NIB= New In Box.
F	None	Metal - trace of rust, some dark patina. Wood - surface smooth, edges slightly rounded.	Makers' marks, if present, are clear and easily legible.
G+	Exact replacement of factory parts	Metal - light rust. Wood - minor surface stress, edges good.	A few dings and/or scratches are O.K.
G	Properly replaced minor parts	Metal - some rust, some minor pitting. Wood - minor chips, shrinkage cracks.	This category represents the average, as-found condition.
G −	Proper major parts, or improper minor parts	Metal - moderate rust, moderate pitting. Wood - warping, chips, minor splitting.	This category definitely indicates a problem. Generally not collectible.
Fr	Improper major parts	Metal - heavy rust and serious pitting, cracks and chips. Wood - warped, large chunks out, major cracks.	May be good for parts.
P	Beyond restoration	Metal - completely rusted and pitted, badly broken. Wood - rot, rough surface, large splits.	Near worthless.

BORING TOOLS

Priced from GOOD to GOOD+

The function of a boring tool is to make a hole, and it must have this working capability to be graded at least as GOOD. The lack of a bit (or drilling piece) will not affect condition since bits are almost always replaceable and were easily separated from the body of the boring tool. Naturally a boring tool has more value if the bit, or a set of bits, are present.

However, a broken chuck that cannot securely hold a bit will downgrade the tool to below GOOD, as will a broken head or handle that affects the tool's ability to function properly.

DRILLS

BOW DRILL

The bow drill consists of two parts: the bow and the drill. Each part should be graded independently of the other. For instance, if a bow drill will not function because of its inability to turn properly or hold a bit, it would be graded less than GOOD even if it had a bow. On the other hand, a perfectly functioning drill in excellent condition, but without a bow, could carry a grading of FINE.

More often than not the bow is either replaced or missing altogether. It is not difficult to see the mismatch of a replaced bow. The handles of the two pieces will be different; and even if they are close in shape, the drill will have obvious age and the bow will not. Where a bow accompanies the drill, the price of the drill is affected as follows:

Unmatched bow and drill, add 25-50% to the drill price.

Matched bow and drill (rarely found), add 50-100% to the drill price.

For each replaceable pad add $10-20.

Many bow drills have heavy cracks in their spindles, particularly if the spindles are made of ivory or ebony. This will put its grade at the lower end of the range. Light checks are acceptable for GOOD. The bit can be missing for GOOD so long as the chuck can accept and hold a replaced bit. If the bow is tightened with a ratcheting mechanism, it is usually worth more than the drill.

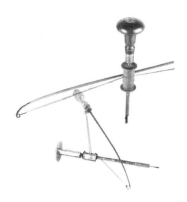

Smooth spindle, shown with bow but
  priced for drill only
  wood spindle, manufactured, *top,* $60-120.
  wood spindle, primitive, $35-70.
  brass spindle and head, *bottom,* $75-150.
  iron spindle, $50-100.

6

Grooved spindle, drill only

    ebony, *top,* $125-225.

    ivory, *bottom,* $225-400.

    rosewood, similar to ebony, $100-200.

    brass, similar to ivory, $175-300.

    Note: An extremely well-made ivory drill with matching

    bow, by J. Most (rare New York City maker), sold in 1995 for $3520.

PUMP DRILL

    Primitive, homemade drills (even those made in the 19th century) can be found looking as if they came from a caveman's toolbox. Size and craftsmanship are the price variables. Fine craftsmanship and unusually large size carry higher prices. A missing or replaced string or thong will not prevent a pump drill from grading GOOD.

Brass or iron flywheel, factory made

    under 15" high, $30-60.

    15" high or over, $50-100.

Wood, stone, or iron flywheel, primitive

    under 15" high, $60-120.

    15" high or over, $80-160.

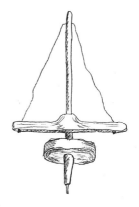

ARCHIMEDEAN DRILL   (also used as a screwdriver)

    The condition of GOOD here is based on the smoothness of the reciprocating motion. No more than a slight "stickiness" is allowed. Checks in wood are acceptable, and where nickel or tin has been plated over brass, some or all of the plating can be worn off. The price range is based mostly upon aesthetic appeal.

Wood center grip and head, *lst left,* $15-30.

Yankee number 50, *4th left,* $40-80.

Patented, "Reid," *2nd left,* $30-60.

Brass center grip and head, *3rd left,* $50-100.

Push drill, "Yankee" style. As this is still a working tool, the price depends on the bits available (usually stored in the handle) and the smoothness of motion, *5th left,* $8-25.

Push drill, plated. Price based mostly on aesthetics of the finish, e.g., no plating at all with the brass showing is better than half the plating off, tarnished, etc., *far right,* $10-20.

All wood (center grip sometimes wrapped with cane or reed), $65-135.

Wood center grip and head, 2 ball flywheel, *top right,* $40-80.

Brass center grip and head, 2 ball flywheel, *center,* $60-120.

Iron center grip and head, 2 ball flywheel, similar to brass above, $40-80.

Center handle, large brass flywheel, *bottom left,* $60-120.

Center handle, without flywheel, $40-80.

BEVEL-GEARED DRILL

To be considered GOOD these drills must maintain the functional smoothness of their gears (slight stickiness is acceptable). Missing handles downgrade the drill. Original paint, particularly if it is decorative, increases the value at least 50%.

Elaborate gear wheel, unusual grip and chuck, *right,* $65-150.

Curved spoke gear wheel, all metal grip, *center,* $35-70.

Jeweler's drill, *left,* $30-60.

Hand drill, wood grip, 3-jaw chuck, $10-25.

    The more bits in the handle, the higher the price.

    Some rare Stanley models go considerably higher.
See John Walter's Price Guide.

"C"-style body casting, wood head and handle,
    $85-175.

Brass-framed drill, $75-150.

Iron-framed drill,

    similar to brass above, $50-100.

Cast iron breast drill, $20-60,

    depending on size and number of gear speeds.

Corner drill - see Corner brace
    (under METAL BODY BRACE, pg. 16)

International Mfg. Co. patent drill, $50-100.

AUGERS and REAMERS

    Most T-augers and reamers (handles fitting crosswise at the top of the bit) are judged mainly by the aesthetics of the handle, i.e., shape, condition and patina, and the degree of rust on the bit. Naturally size plays a role also; the larger ones bring the most money. GOOD condition allows complete oxidation of the bit but no flaking rust or pitting. Normal cracks and wear of the handle are acceptable but the handle must hold the bit firmly and the bit must not have any part of its tip broken away.

Shipwright's breast auger
primitive, *right,* $65-135.
turned, more ornate, $100-200.

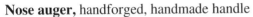

Nose auger, handforged, handmade handle
1" diameter, *right top,* $20-40.
½" diameter, $15-30.

Spiral auger
bulbous handle, 3" dia., double fluted,
 center, $25-50.
single fluted, ³/4" dia., handle through end ring,
 bottom, $8-15.
factory turned handle, double fluted, *right*
  3" dia., $20-40.
  1½" dia., $10-20.
  ½" dia., $8-15.

Handforged square or octagonal shanks are valued at the top of
the range.

Patent quick release, handle only, $12-25.

Gimlet
shipwright's gimlet, *top left,* $5-10.
bell hanger's gimlet, *second from top,* $10-20.
carpenter's factory-made gimlet, *center bottom,*
 $4-8.
shell type gimlet (with spiral tip), *far right,* $6-12.

Beam boring machine
For GOOD, the catch that holds the frame up (prior to drilling) can be
missing, as this does not hamper drilling. However the chuck and
gear rack must be workable.
adjustable model, *right,* $85-225.
adjustable model with metal upright rods, $125-300.
fixed model (one vertical position only), $65-150.

Pipe auger, nose bit *(left)* and pipe reamer, spoon bit *(right)*
These are used with a removeable iron T-handle and are usually
2" - 6" diameter, with some pitting. A rough estimate is $7-15 per
inch of diameter.

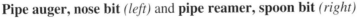

Cooper's reamer
8" overall length,
handshaped handle, *top,* $8-15.
turned handle, *bottom,* $10-20.
18" overall length, $25-60.

Wheelwright's reamer
approx. 30" overall length, 3" diameter, turned handle, *center,* $50-100.

Hooked reamer
same as wheelwright's reamer except a hook at the bottom end, $65-150. (Some are used with a removeable metal handle, which is almost always missing.)

Cooper's bung hole borer
3" diameter, $15-30.
2" diameter, $12-25.

BRACES

Braces are divided into three categories:

1. Primitives, all wood, craftsman-made—The bits permanently fit into wooden pads that are removeable from the nose of the brace. These are the earliest, a good many from the 18th century.

2. Sheffield style, manufactured—Utilizing metal and wood; a brass chuck, reinforcing brass plates or brass frames, and sometimes a brass neck to attach the revolving head to the body. These generally date from late 18th century to late 19th century.

3. Metal body—The earlier varieties are handforged with little or no wooden parts. Factory-made models (mostly patented) became dominant after the mid-19th century, with little change after 1900.

PRIMITIVE BRACE

For a primitive brace to be considered GOOD it must have:

1. A head that revolves freely, though it may be loose.

2. Body splits must be repaired in a way that maintains the old look. Early repairs using large bolts and nuts to hold the split together are not acceptable. Generally screwed-on metal plates used for repair or reinforcement are acceptable.

3. Significant worm or any rot is not acceptable, but a "weathered" look is.

4. The original pads are seldom found with the brace. A replacement pad or no pad at all does not degrade the brace's condition, though it will bring it to a lower level of the price range. However, all the primitive braces below are priced as if they have one original pad. For extra replacement pads, add $8-15; for extra original pads add $15-30. A replacement pad usually has at least one of the following errors:

wrong shape (doesn't follow style of body),

wrong fit (taper doesn't coincide between pad and body), or

mismatched patina (most common).

Primitive braces are valued mostly for eye-appealing shapes and pleasing patina.

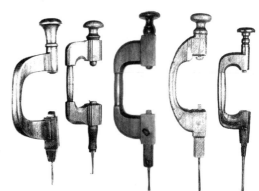

Scandanavian, tilted grip, *left,* $100-200.

Austrian, *second from left,* $75-150.

Common shape, *center,* $75-150.

Graceful, *far right,* $100-200.

Early arch grip, *2nd from right,* $100-200.

Ornate, e.g., tiger maple, carvings, etc. $150-350.

Primitive looking, $35-75.

Dutch, with removeable pad, *left,* $75-150.

Dutch, with fixed bit, *right,* $40-75.

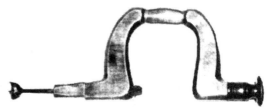

Massive size, 20" overall (including pad but not bit), 7" throw (centerline of grip to centerline of bit and head), $150-350.

Note: A signed brace of this approximate size (made by planemaker E. W. Carpenter) with 9 pads sold for $5000 at auction.

Transitional style, $75-150.

English boatsway, $60-120.

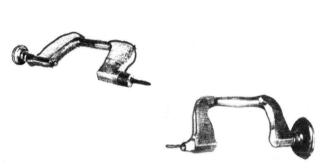

Chairmaker's brace, $75-150.

Cooper's brace, $150-250.

Note: Because of their greater availability in England, chairmaker's, cooper's, boatsways, and Dutch braces tend to sell in English auctions for somewhat less than shown above.

Pianomaker's brace, $225-450.

Not truly a primitive brace. It has the Sheffield style profile to the body (although much smaller), but its chuck is merely a round tapered hole taking pads.

Note: An Erlandsen (N. Y. maker) pianomaker's brace of rosewood, with 3 matching pads sold privately in1991 for $3500.

SHEFFIELD STYLE

These braces can be further broken down into Sheffield-unplated (without side reinforcing brass plates), Sheffield-plated (with reinforcing plates), and Brass-framed (with wood infills) commonly called "Ultimatum-style".

To qualify for GOOD these braces must have a functioning chuck, i.e., the button, lever or ring used to retain the bit must be complete and working. If the head will not turn, or in the case of the Brass-framed style, the wrist grip is jammed, this reduces it to the bottom of the range. Looseness between the head and body is acceptable as GOOD and in most cases can be easily corrected. In the Brass-framed style slight rock between the wrist grip and the webs is also acceptable, even though it is difficult to correct. Checks are common throughout the ebony parts of the Brass-framed style. They are generally accepted as GOOD unless they significantly affect appearance. A missing head button or trade disk, or a replaced head, relegates the brace to GOOD MINUS. However a replacement ivory ring on the Brass-framed style is acceptable as GOOD or GOOD PLUS.

The chucks that are activated with levers are rarer and are valued 10-20% higher.

Some of the more important Sheffield-style brace makers are listed on the next page. Those with asterisks will be found at the higher end of the price range.

James Bee, Henry Brown, Brown & Flather, *J. Cooper, Henry Dixon, *Fenton & Marsden, Flather & Son, D. Flather, James Howarth, Thomas Ibbotson, *William Marples, *Robert Marples, *Marsden Bros., Marsh Bros., A. Mathieson, Moulson Bros., *Henry Pasley, Alfred Ridge, Joseph Slater, I. Sorby, *Tillotson, *Thomas Turner, and F. Walter.

Unplated, beech body
> unsigned, $50-100.
> signed, $60-120.
> with chuck button on right side, $65-135.

Plated, beech body
> unsigned, head and neck lignum, $65-135.
> signed
>> head and neck lignum, $75-150.
>> head ebony, neck brass, *right,* $100-200.
>> with registry numbers, $125-250.
>> by American makers such as Booth & Mills, T.E. Wells (large letters in a straight line), or J.T. Jones, $150-300.

Plated, ebony body, similar to plated beech body above, $400-750.

C & T Pilkington, $800-1500.
> There are variations of the signature. This brace is inscribed "By Her Majesty's Royal Letters Patent".

Brass-framed, "Ultimatum-style"

The term "trade brace" was used to designate a brace made for distributors, without the maker's name on the brace. It usually carries a trade disk on the head that reads "Warranted Superior." The only braces that carry the inscription "Ultimatum" are those of William or Robert Marples, and the only one of those inscribed "By Her Majesty's Royal Letters Patent" is William Marples'. Although there are more William Marples brass framed braces than those of any other manufacturer, his braces are in the upper portion of the value range because of the inscriptions.

> Trade brace in ebony, $225-325.
> Signed by a maker
>> ebony, *right,* $275-375.
>> beech, $350-475.
>> rosewood, $600-1000.
>> horn, $800-1600.
>> boxwood, $1500-3000.

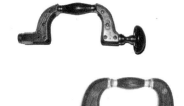

> Sims-style brass-framed, $1200-2000
> There are a variety of signatures on this type brace.

As with all tools, a slight difference in model sometimes means a significant difference in price. *At an English auction, a beech Ultimatum with a "short nozzle" sold for $2718.* Refer to the description of the various types and their makers in Reg Eaton's *The Ultimate Brace* (see Bibliography).

METAL BODY BRACE

These braces fall into two main groups: the early handforged blacksmith-made ones and the later, mostly patented, factory-made ones.

The most common missing part in either group is the chuck thumbscrew. This generally downgrades the brace to GOOD MINUS.

Most of the heads are quite loose in the handforged models, and in some cases the head button is missing. Neither of these problems prevent the GOOD rating.

The patina in the handforged braces (particularly the cagehead models), is very dark, actually approaching black. Don't try to remove this and "shine it up"; it will reduce its value. Workmanship (chamfers, grace of design, etc.) is what adds value to these old handforged braces, while rarity is the key to increased value in the patented factory-made braces.

A "folding" patent brace by Stites (1905) in FINE condition sold for $7000 in a 2000 auction.

Blacksmith-made brace

    lathe-turned wood head, iron ferrule, *right*, $30-60.
    hand-carved wood head, *center,* $20-35.
    long graceful sweep, turned wood head, brass ferrule, *left,*
        $40-90.

metal head, $25-50.

blacksmith beam brace, $35-70.

European

handforged, all iron brace, ogee offset to front arm, *top,* $200-400.
handforged, brass grip and head, *bottom,* $150-250.

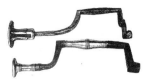

Cage head

2 bars, *right,* $75-150.
3 bars, $85-175.
4 bars, $100-200.

Corner brace

Rusby patent, $30-60.

Millers Falls patent, *right,* $35-70.
Stanley, similar to Millers Falls, $50-100.

Gent's or Six-penny brace, $30-60.

Fray patent with Spofford chuck

wooden grip and head, *right,* $30-70.
metal grip and head, $15-35.

Scotch wagon brace, $35-70.

American wagon brace, $15-30.

Some patented models could go as high as $150.   See *The American Patent Brace* by Ron Pearson.

Whimble brace, $50-100.

Taylor patent, *left*, $25-50.

Staples, *center*, $50-100.

Davis Level & Tool Co. patent, *right,* $50-100.

Lowentraut patent (combination wrench and brace),
$65-125.

Ordnance brace, entirely of brass, $50-100.

Hollow auger brace, $40-75.

Patented brace chucks,
shown from left to right:
Hildreth 1870, $60-125.
Stackpole 1867, $75-150.
Daboll 1868, $50-100.
Nobles 1865, $35-75.
Shepardson 1870, $60-175.
Stackpole 1862, $75-150.
Holt 1880, $20-50.
Chantrell 1883, $125-250.
B. Darling 1868, *right,* $400-800.

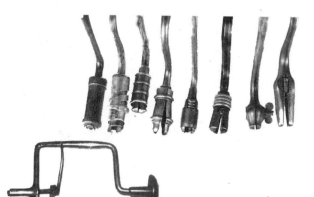

Other brace patents for chucks or ratchets are on the next page. (See *The American Patent Brace*
by Ron Pearson.)

Patents for chucks or ratchets,
> Peck, Stow & Wilcox 1879, $40-80
> Shepard 1884, $40-80
> Backus 1872 or 1880, $30-60
> Bolen 1886, $40-80
> Amidon 1868, $35-70
> Amidon 1883, $50-100
> Peck 1879, $60-150
> Smith, H.V. 1883, $80-175

Millers Falls, *right,* $8-25.
> Other similar patents can go as high as $200. (See *The American Patent Brace* by Ron Pearson.)

Stanley, similar to above, $10-35.
> See John Walter's book for the less common Stanley braces. They can go as high as $150.

Horton, brass body and head, rosewood grip, $600-1200.

Palmer patent washer cutter, $60-120.

Surgeon's brace, $50-100.

> Ornate surgeon's braces with ebony heads and grips sell as high as $500.

Bits
> (Higher prices for larger sizes); from left to right:
> 1) spiral - less than $1-2 (unless in sets); 2) center - $2-5; 3) reamer - $2-5; 4) nose - $3-10; 5) shell - $1-3; 6) spoon - $2-8.
> Very large sizes and specialty bits can go as high as $35. Sets of matched spiral bits in their original box sell for $50-100.

1   2   3   4   5   6

> Spoke pointer, *right,* $10-20.
> Tenon cutter or Hollow auger
>> adjustable, *left,* $30-75.
>> fixed, $12-30.

EDGE TOOLS

Priced from GOOD to GOOD+

Edge tools are comparatively simple to grade for condition as they have substantially only two parts, the blade and the handle.

Handles are often replaced over the life of the tool. Whether they are *early* proper replacements or originals is difficult to establish and makes little difference in price. Any proper replacement handle is acceptable for the grade of GOOD. An original or early replacement with cracks or checks, or one that is loose, also qualifies for GOOD. However, heavy pitting, significant metal cracks, or excessive wear of the blade will downgrade the tool to GOOD MINUS or below.

A "laid-on" steel edge has more value than the later all-cast or all-forged steel blades. The laid-on demarcation line is almost always visible on one side at least.

For tools without handles, or handles nearly worthless, reduce the pricing estimate by $1/3$ to $1/2$.

Those edge tools that are signed will generally be at the upper end of the grade price range. In the case of desireable makers, the price could go above the top of the range.

AXES

FELLING AXE

Single bit

> common pattern, *bottom*, $10-20.
> with embossing, $50-100.
> early pattern, *center right*, $20-40.
> Rockaway pattern (McKinnon *Co.*), *top left*, $15-30.

Double bit

> with embossing, *right*, $65-200, based on the details of the embossing.
> without embossing, $12-25.

BROAD AXE

Pennsylvania pattern, *left,* $50-100.
Canada pattern, *right*, $50-100.

New England pattern,
   left, $35-75.

New Orleans pattern,
   center, $50-100.

Western pattern,
   right, $50-100.

GOOSEWING AXE

European style, socket parallel to blade, handle curved up, eye over $\frac{3}{8}$" wide, *left,* $150-350, depending on degree of decoration.

American style, socket bent up from blade, handle straight, eye under $\frac{3}{8}$" wide.
         unsigned or illegible, *right,* $175-375.
         signed, $275-600, depending greatly on the maker.
   Note: Some of the desireable Pennsylvania makers' signatures are Sener, Brady, Addams, Stohler, Stahler, Rohrbach and Beatty.

Austrian style, depending on size and decorativeness, $300-800.

SHIPWRIGHT'S AXE

   Kent style, *left,* $35-75.
   Mast axe, *right,* $50-100.

COOPER'S AXE

   $45-90.

COACHMAKER'S AXE

Bearded, *left,* $65-150.

Standard European style, *right,* $75-175.

ICE AXE

   $25-50.
   Note: There are many patterns of ice axes, all having a pike on the rear end of the head. Pricing is about the same.

FIRE AXE

Early, embossed, *right,* $150-300.

Early, unembossed, similar in shape to above, $100-200.

Later, modern style, $15-30.

MORTISING AXE

Stepped blade, *bottom,* $45-100.

Standard blade, *top,* $30-70.

Double-bladed, $65-125.

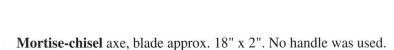

Mortise-chisel axe, blade approx. 18" x 2". No handle was used.
$125-225.

Note: To emphasize the importance of a signature in proving provenance (in this case establishing an American-made tool), a Pennsylvania mortise-chisel axe by a local maker (J. Dubs) sold at auction for $1850. Normally almost all of these axes are of European origin.

TRADE AXE

(Decorativeness is an important price factor.)

Squaw axe, *top,* $60-120.

Standard pattern
handforged, *bottom,* $45-90.
cast, similar to above, $30-60.

TURF or BOG AXE

(Blade too thin to cut wood.)

Riveted style, *top,* $30-70.

Forged style, similar to above, $40-90.

Sleigh pattern, *bottom*, $75-150.

HATCHET

Lathing, $7-15.

Utility (shingling), *bottom,* $8-20.

Camper's, *top,* $10-25.

Hewing (one side completely flat, 6" - 8" edge, similar to a small broad axe), $20-40.

Marble Safety Axe Co., with protective edge cover, $75-150.

ADZES

Although adzes are still used today in timber framing and shipbuilding, the older ones are bought mostly for their graceful form. The greater the curvature of the handle, the more appealing and the more valuable they are.

CARPENTER'S ADZE

Poll-less (i.e., without protrusion on rear end)
  head length 10" or over, *center,* $25-50.
  head length under 10", $15-35.

Hammerhead poll, *right,* $20-40.

SHIPWRIGHT'S ADZE

With rolled up "lips" (on sides of head),
  left, $25-50.

Without lips, $20-40.

GUTTER or HOLLOWING ADZE

With short poll, *left,* $25-50.

With long poll, *center,* $35-75.

Poll-less, *right,* $20-40.

HAND ADZE

Stirrup or Strap Adze

closed or "D" handle, *left,* $60-120.
closed handle, decorative carving, $100-250.
open handle, decorative carving, *right,* $75-200.
open handle, no carving, $40-80.

Cooper's Adze

handforged, early, *left,* $20-40.
factory-made, *right*, $30-60.

Bowl Adze

up to 3" wide, *left*, $50-100.
3" - 5" wide, $60-125.
over 5" wide, $80-175.
French style, *right*, $100-200.

CHISELS

(Including gouges and other shapes)

These are perhaps the most utilitarian of all the tools in the "antique" class. The steel in the blade is the most important variable for value. It is difficult to tell the actual hardness of the steel without experience (some can do it with the pitch of the sound when running a file across it). Some people have the notion that older steel was made better than the steel used in chisels today. It's hard to endorse such a sweeping generality. Though common department store chisels may not match the earlier ones, high quality contemporary ones do.

There are some obvious deficiencies that can be spotted quickly, such as heavy pitting or heavy wear down. Neither are acceptable for the GOOD grade.

Handles, though much less important than the quality of the blade, do have an effect on price. Something that looks as if you should pick it up and start using it will have much more value attached to it. As such, tools with well formed handles of boxwood or rosewood will bring 50% to 100% more than those with plainer handles. The price estimates are based on proper hardwood handles of the plainer variety.

In a similar size and quality, a gouge (concave cross-section) will bring more than a flat chisel; a bent or crank-neck shank more than a straight shank, and a dished or spoon-shaped tip more than a straight tip. Even though smaller in size, carving tools are more sought after and more expensive than lathe-turning tools.

Firmer chisels, or any other type designed to be struck with a mallet, are downgraded to the lower end of the range if they are missing their striking ring or end ferrule. Some have composition ends, or specially turned ends, to keep them from splitting. These types do not have end ferrules.

In almost all types of chisels and gouges, the larger sizes are more expensive. An exception is very small sizes of carving tools; these bring premiums of 50% or more. For all types, matched sets bring approximately 25% more.

Some quality makers in this country were: D.R. Barton, Buck Bros., Douglas Mfg. Co., C.E. Jennings, James Swan, L. & I.J. White, and T.H. Witherby; and in England were: S.J. Addis, Butcher, Ibbotson, Marples, Moulson Bros., I. Sorby, and Ward.

FIRMER, FRAMING or STRAIGHT CHISEL

The terms firmer and framing are generally used for the heavier, longer chisels. Some have a socket at the end of the blade into which the handle is friction fitted. These socket chisels run 14" - 17" in over-all length.

A lighter, smaller type of straight chisel, usually called a "bench" chisel, has the tang of the blade driven into the handle and a ferrule used to keep the handle from splitting. These normally run 8" - 12" in over-all length.

Socket-fitted handle
square sides, *top and bottom,* $7-20.
beveled sides, *center,* $10-25.

Stanley "Everlast," $20-60.
Most Everlast sets run over $500.

Tang-fitted handle
square sides, $6-12.

beveled sides, $10-20.

PARING CHISEL and PARING GOUGE

(not intended to be struck with a mallet)

Paring chisel, beveled sides
straight shank, *top,* $8-15.
bent shank, $12-25.

Paring gouge
straight shank, $12-25.
bent shank, *bottom,* $15-30.

GOUGE

Socket-fitted, *bottom*, $12-25.

Tang-fitted, *top*, $10-20.

MORTISE CHISEL

Straight, *top,* $12-25.

Goosenecked, *bottom*, $30-75.

Twybill

> French, 48" long. No handle was used.
> $150-250.

> Pennsylvanian (from German origin), under 36".
> Used with a handle. $175-300.

CORNER CHISEL

Standard 90° angle, $25-50.

Primitive bruzz, approx. 60°, *top*, $15-30 .

Factory-made bruzz, approx. 60°, *bottom*, $20-40.

SLICK or SHIPWRIGHT'S CHISEL

Many slicks have handles that are not proper. Slicks were designed not to be struck but pushed, and usually have rounded palm grips at their handle ends rather than a ferrule or striking ring. Improper handles downgrade the slick approximately 25%.

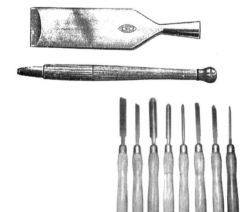

Blade width
> 2" - 2$\frac{1}{2}$", $40-80.
> 2¾," - 3", $60-120.
> 3$\frac{1}{2}$", $75-150.
> 4", $90-175.

TURNING TOOLS

Set of 8, $40-80.

Turner's sizing tool, $50-100.

CARVING TOOLS

Standard handles are shown on the left three tools. Fancy handles are shown on the right two tools. Prices below are for standard handles. Add 25-50% for fancy turned handles and another 25-50% for boxwood or rosewood handles.

Straight chisel (edge 90° to shank), $5-10.

Skew chisel (edge skewed diagonally to shank), $5-10.

Gouge (U-shaped cross section), $8-15.

Fluter (deeper U than gouge), $10-20.

Veiner (higher sides than fluter), $12-25.

V-parting tool (V-shaped cross section), *center*, $12-25.

Spoon gouge (spoonlike tip), *right*, $15-30.

Back bent gouge (cutting edge upside-down), *second from right*, $10-20.

Bent gouge (lengthwise bend to the blade), *left*, $10-20.

Fishtail gouge (fanned out at tip), $12-25.

KNIVES

Knives have about the same grading criteria as chisels.

DRAW KNIFE

Carpenter's
> approx. 15" over all, *left,* $15-35.
> 6" - 10" over all, $25-70.
> under 6", $35-90.

Cooper's, curved, *right,* $30-75.

Adjustable handle
> with guide, *bottom,* $45-100.
> without guide, $25-70.

Mast knife, approx. 24"- 30" over all
> (similar to carpenter's draw knife), $45-100.

"Gent's," fancy turned handles, brass ferrules, $35-85.

SCORP

Closed
> one-handed, *left,* $15-30.
> two-handed, *center*, $20-40.

Open, *right,* $20-40.

Box scraper (factory-made, shallow curvature), $15-30.

COOPER'S CHAMFER KNIFE

Blade width
> 4" - 5", $25-45.
> 5" - 6", $35-65.

CABINETMAKER'S KNIFE

Ebony and brass handle, $20-40.

Mahogany and brass handle, $15-30.

BLOCK or BENCH KNIFE

Hook end, T-handle, 24" - 36", $50-100.

RACE KNIFE

Double blade, $40-100.

Single blade
> curved shank, $20-45.

> brass holder, blade foldable, $15-35.

FROE or RIVING KNIFE

Straight, *right*, $25-45.

Curved, *left*, $60-120.

BARK SPUD   (most do not have "D" handles)

Spatula tip, handforged, *top*, $20-40.

Spade tip, handforged, *center*, $20-40.

Swage tip, handforged, *bottom*, $15-30.

Hook tip, factory-made, $25-50.

CROOKED KNIFE

Ornate carving and inlay work, *top*,
(characteristics of folk art), $200-400.

With carvings, but no inlay, *bottom*, $150-300,
based upon detail.

Standard wire or string wrapped,
no carving or inlays, $40-80.

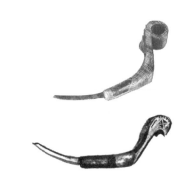

Note: In a 1991 American Indian art auction, a crooked knife, with the curved portion of the handle carved into a horse's head and neck, and a tiny carved rider mounted on the straight portion, sold for $27,500! It was described as an important piece of effigy sculpture.

CLOGGER'S KNIFE

(for making wooden shoes)

36"- 44" over-all,
each at right, $40-90.

BUTTRESS   (farrier's hoof trimmer)

Simple, *top*, $18-35.

Reverse turned with shoulder butt handle,
bottom, $30-60.

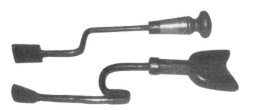

Note: An extremely decorative hand wrought buttress brought $800 in a 1997 auction.

WOODEN PLANES

Priced from GOOD to GOOD+

Considering the hundreds of plane types, thousands of planemaker imprints, and the many variations in condition, all of which combine to determine price, the possible combinations are in the millions!

To achieve a practical answer to this problem American wooden planes are divided into two main sections, each with its own sub-sections.

Section 1. Covers wooden planes without any planemaker or dealer imprint. Care must be taken not to confuse owner imprints with planemaker or dealer marks. The planemaker or dealer imprint is found on the upper front end (the toe) of the plane. Sometimes the mark will include a geographic location. Owners' names, and initials, will be found almost anywhere on the plane, often stamped several times and hardly ever showing a geographic location. You can check the name against the **Planemaker's Directory** included in this *Price Guide*, starting on page 47, or for a more complete listing refer to *A Guide to the Makers of American Wooden Planes* for American wooden plane makers and to *British Planemakers Since 1700* for English planemakers. See the Bibliography for details.

Section 2. (See page 46). Covers American wooden planes with a planemaker or dealer imprint. In this section over 400 different planemakers are priced by type of plane. These imprints include the most important early makers and the more prolific later ones, and cover the majority of planes normally seen.

Characteristics for *at least* a GOOD condition grade for wooden planes are:

1. The body may show normal use and patina; i.e., there may be cracks, checks, chips, dents, nicks, or stains, and some wear on the sole, but these defects are not obtrusive.

2. No rot. If there are worm holes, they are minimal (close to unnoticeable).

3. There is an appropriate cutting iron in the plane.

4. If boxed (wear strips in the sole), the boxing is intact and functional. It may be replaced if properly done.

5. Slight looseness or binding of parts is acceptable.

6. The cutter wedge should be original or a proper replacement. The wedge finial should not be sheared. See *Guide to the Makers of American Wooden Planes* (Bibliography) for correct wedge shapes.

7. The plane should not be recut or shortened.

8. If there is a maker's imprint, it should be legible.

9. Screw or slide arms should be moveable. Thread chipping or stripping should be minimal and not obtrusive. Arm wedges, thumbscrews, and nuts should be original or proper replacements.

10. Depth stops should be complete and in working order.

11. Nickers and nicker wedges should be original or proper replacements.

12. Handle tips should be largely intact or properly and unobtrusively repaired.

13. Metal parts can show minor rust or pitting.

14. Wooden parts can show minor stains or weathering.

SECTION 1

Wooden Planes Without a Planemaker or Dealer Imprint

The prices shown in this section are for planes made after 1800, unless otherwise stated. Planes have certain characteristics that may help to indicate their age. Some of these characteristics as they pertain to American planes are:

1. The length of the plane. Molding planes went to a standard 9½" length during the second quarter of the 19th century. Generally the longer the plane, the earlier it is. Planes 9⅞"-10" long probably date before the American Revolution; 9⅝"-9¾" indicates the last quarter of the 18th century to the early 19th century. Planes are sometimes found less than 9½" long, usually between 9¼"-9⅜". These usually date from around 1800.

2. The kind of chamfering (finish of the edges) the plane has along its top and down the sides of its toe and heel. Wide flat chamfers (⅜"- ½") usually appear on planes made before 1800. Narrower flat chamfers (³⁄₁₆" - ¼") indicate circa 1800. Wide rounded chamfers (¼" - ⅜") usually appear on planes made between 1800 and 1830. After that, narrow rounded chamfers (⅛" - ³⁄₁₆") or no chamfers became the standard.

3. The kind of wood that was used. Yellow birch usually means a plane made before 1800. Beech was used both early and late. Ebony, boxwood, rosewood, and lignum vitae usually indicate a date well after 1800.

4. On plow planes, riveted skates are early, usually before 1800; screwed skates after 1800. Screw arms appeared after 1800, most frequently after 1830. Slide arms were used on both early and late planes.

As a rule of thumb, 18th century unimprinted planes are valued around double the prices shown for unimprinted planes in this section (Section 1).

BENCH PLANES

Bench planes are probably the most frequently found of the wooden planes. They were one of the most important basic tools used by the woodworker. Because of their availability and low cost, they are among the first tools acquired by many collectors. Interestingly these attractive tools, often over 100 years old, sell for much less than modern reproductions designed for use by contemporary woodworkers. However, there is considerable interest shown in these appealing tools by the general antique and decorating markets. Consequently a premium is paid for attractive over-all appearance and a discount taken if the plane appears dirty or lifeless. The price range for bench planes averages out this market bias.

As a general rule, early bench planes will have flat chamfers, late, rounded; early bench planes with handles will have the handle offset to one side, late will be centered; original irons in early bench planes will have arched or rounded tops, later irons will be squared off. Early types tend to fall in the higher end of their respective price ranges.

SMOOTH PLANE, 6½ " - 10½" long

A

Unhandled, *A-bottom*
    beech, $6-12.
    apple or mahogany, $20-40.
    lignum, $30-60.
    boxwood or rosewood, $40-80.
    ebony, $60-120.

Handled, razee, (stepped body), *B*
    beech, $12-25.
    apple or mahogany, $30-60.
    lignum, $40-80.
    boxwood or rosewood, $60-120.
    ebony, $75-150.

B

JACK PLANE, 14" - 16" long

Standard body, *A-second from bottom*
    beech, $10-20.

Razee body, *C-bottom next page*
    beech, $12-25.
    apple or mahogany, $30-60.
    lignum, $40-80.
    rosewood, $60-120.
    ebony, $100-200.

FORE PLANE, 18" - 22" long

Standard body, *A- second from top prev. pg.*
    beech, $12-22.

Razee body, *C-middle*
    beech, $18-30.
    apple or mahogany, $40-80.
    lignum, $50-100.
    rosewood, $75-150.
    ebony, $125-225.

C

JOINTER, over 22" long

Standard body, beech, *A-top prev. pg.*
    24"-30", $18-25.
    31"-36", $25-50.
    over 36", $40-80.

Razee body, 24"-30", *C-top*
    beech, $20-35.
    apple or mahogany, $50-100.
    lignum, $75-150.
    rosewood, $100-225.
    ebony, $150-275.

OTHER FINISHING PLANES

MITER PLANE

    left, $10-22.

TOOTHING PLANE

    right, $20-40.

COMPASS PLANE

Fixed, *right,* $15-30.

Adjustable, *left,* $40-75.

MINIATURE SMOOTHER

3" - 6". Generally, the smaller the plane, the more valuable.

        beech, $30-60.
        boxwood, $45-90.

PLANES USED FOR CUTTING JOINTS

RABBET

Unhandled, *left*, $6-10.

Handled, *lower right*, $15-30.

Ship's jack rabbet, *middle,* $30-60.

Jack rabbet (without razee), $25-50.

Side rabbet, $15-30 each,
    (add 25% for matched pairs),
    right- and left-handed.

FILLETSTER

Moving (no arms), $22-45.

Screw arm, handled, $75-175.

Screw arm, unhandled, $60-125.

Slide arm, unhandled, $40-90.

Slide arm, handled, $60-125.

SASH FILLETSTER, unhandled

English screw arm, $85-150.

English slide arm, $60-100.

SASH PLANE, unhandled

Solid body, single iron, *upper left*, $20-40.

Solid body, double iron, *upper right*, $25-50.

Split body, double iron, adjustable screws,
   lower left, $30-60.

Split body, double iron, screw arms,
   lower right, $40-80.

PLOW PLANE

Plow planes, like bench planes, are part of almost everyone's collection. Common plows sell for less than they deserve, as most collectors are looking beyond the "starter" variety. As with bench planes, condition is heavily influenced by aesthetics. Even though a plane may be completely functional, if it is unsigned and crude looking, it will sell below the GOOD category. Broken away handle tips, screws holding cracks together, heavy pitting on the skate, all seriously degrade the plane. And the reverse, a truly superb looking plane can sell for twice the price shown.

A general rule of thumb is to allow $2\frac{1}{2}$ - $3\frac{1}{2}$ times normal pricing for whatever condition category the plane is in when it has proper ivory fence arm tips.

The condition of the arms is perhaps the most important factor in rating the plane. If it has slide arms and they are warped and bound, or the tips are badly battered, the plane will degrade to GOOD MINUS. If it has screw arms and one of the locking nuts is missing, or the threads are stripped in places, it will degrade to GOOD MINUS.

Exotic wood plows tend to be valued by the "look of the wood" rather than the rarity of the maker. The price differential between unnamed and named plows in the exotic woods is considerably less than normally found in other types of planes.

Slide arm, wedged arms, unhandled, beech, $40-75.

Slide arm, thumbscrewed arms, unhandled, beech, $40-75.

Screw arm, unhandled
    beech, $55-100.
    apple or boxwood, $85-175.
    rosewood, $140-275.
    ebony, $400-700.

Screw arm, handled
    beech, $70-135.
    apple or boxwood, $125-275.
    rosewood, $225-400.
    ebony, $500-900.

Plow plane irons
    set of 8, different makers, $40-80.
    set of 8, same maker, English, $60-120.
    set of 8, same maker, American, $70-140.

Yankee type plow, square slide arms, *right*, $75-175.

SPECIAL TYPES OF PLOW PLANES

Bridle plow (English)
    unhandled, $100-200.
    handled, $150-275.

Kimberly patent bridle plow (English)
    unhandled, *right,* $150-225.
    handled, $200-300.

Continental European plow
left, $50-100.
right, $45-85.

AMERICAN PATENTED WOODEN PLOWS

Israel White patented three-arm plow, $3500-5500.
Note: A rare model of this plow with ivory tipped ebony arms and an ivory scale set into the arm, sold at auction for $12,500 in 1997.

E.W. Carpenter.
There are a series of four Carpenter "patent" imprints that refer to the improved arms and handles of the plow planes. These planes, made of beech or a combination of boxwood and rosewood, are very impressive looking, and much sought after by collectors.

beech,
> unhandled, $1200-2000.
> handled, $2500-4500.

boxwood and rosewood,
> unhandled, $2000-3500.
> handled, $3500-5500.

Chapin-Rust self-adjusting patented three-arm plow, handled
$1500-3000.
There are 2 other variations of this patent. The *metal* bridle model is valued at the high end of the range.

Sandusky center wheel plow, handled
brass center wheel
> boxwood, $3000-4500.
> rosewood, $4000-6000.

An ivory-tipped rosewood model in G+ condition sold for $16,500 in a 1997 auction, and an ivory-tipped boxwood model in FINE condition sold for $20,000 in a 2000 auction.

Ohio Tool center wheel plow, handled, similar to Sandusky above except that the center wheel is wood rather than brass.
> boxwood, $2500-4000.
> rosewood, $3500-5500.

DADO PLANE

Wood stop, *right,* $12-22.

Metal thumbscrew stop, *left,* $12-25.

Side stop (metal stop on the side of the plane
    adjusted with a wood screw), $12-25.

TONGUE & GROOVE MATCH PLANES

(priced individually; add *25%* for matched pairs)

Unhandled, *left,* $8-15, each.

Handled, $15-25, each.

Combination, *right*, $25-45.

Plank plane, handled

    friction slide arm, *pair at right,* $40-80, each.
    wedge slide arm (similar to above except for wedges
    locking the arm to the body), $20-40, each.

    screw arm (only tongue plane shown), $30-50, each.

PLANES USED FOR CUTTING DECORATIVE SHAPES

Planes in this category constitute the largest group of wooden planes used by today's woodworkers. Collectors and users often compete for the same planes. Planes with the more common maker imprints and those that are unsigned are readily bought by the user, whose major criteria are "how well will it cut" and "do I need that particular profile in that size?" Consequently, a simple bead (a plane that almost every collector owns) will be sought after by the user if it is a size he needs. On the other hand, a set of four signed rosewood molders sold for $2000 to a collector because they were spectacular in both appearance and condition, aside from the rarity of the rosewood.

Other variables that affect the price of planes in this category are the width of the cut, the complexity of the profile, and the extent to which boxing (wear strips in the sole) is used.

Bead planes in sets particularly attract users, as do hollows and rounds. Most collectors do not look for working sets, with the possible exception of the hollows and rounds.

HOLLOW and ROUND

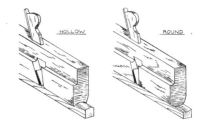

$6-12, each.

Set of 18 (9 matched pairs)
English, $250-450.
American, $300-525.

BEAD

Side bead
single boxing, *left,* $8-15.
full boxing, i.e., the entire profile is cut into the boxing, $10-20.

Center bead
double boxing, *right,* $10-20.
full boxing, $12-25.

ASTRAGAL

$12-30.

OVOLO

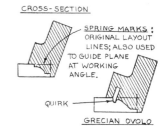

Note: Width refers to the cutting edge of the plane iron.
under 1¼ " wide, $12-30.
1¼ " and over wide, $20-45.

COVE (cavetto or scotia)

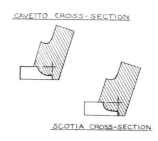

$12-30.

OGEE

Note: Width refers to the cutting edge of the iron.
under 1¼ " wide, $15-35.
1¼ " and over wide, $20-50.

COMPLEX MOLDING PLANE

Complex molders with extremely intricate or very wide profiles command a premium of 50%. Note: Width refers to the cutting edge of the iron.

Unhandled

under 1¼" wide, $25-60.
1¼" - 1¾" wide, $35-75.
over 1¾" wide, $50-125.

double iron, $75-150.

triple iron, *left,* $175-350.
quadruple iron, *right,* $300-600.

Handled

double iron, $150-300.
triple iron, $300-600.

CORNICE, CROWN MOLDER, or HANDLED MOLDER

As with plow planes, price is greatly affected by aesthetics and over-all appearance; e.g., even though the plane is completely functional with only minor defects, if it is crude looking, it may sell as if it were in the GOOD MINUS category. Extremely complex or unusual profiles command a premium. Very few have the front pull handle as shown. Most have a hole through the body, so the helper can pull the plane with a rope. *Note: Width refers to the cutting edge of the iron.*

2", $70-150.
2½", $90-185.
3", $125-235.
4", $200-325.

Cornice planes or crown molders with irons over 4" wide at the cutting edge are rare and sell for proportionally much more.

PLANES USED FOR CUTTING FUNCTIONAL SHAPES

PANEL RAISER

Integral fence (early), $100-200.

Adjustable fence
  sliding fences, *right,* 3" iron, $85-150.
  screw arms, *left,* 3" iron, $125-225.

GUTTER PLANE

$15-25.

PUMP LOG PLANE

$25-50.

CHAMFER PLANE

$50-100.

NOSING PLANE

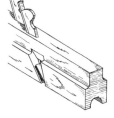

Double iron, *at right,* $20-45.
Single iron, $15-30.

SPECIALIZED PLANES

COOPER'S JOINTER

Single throat

    3', $50-90.

    4', $60-120.

    5', $100-200.

    6', $125-250.

Double throat

    3', $70-120.

    4', $90-175.

    5', $125-225.

    6', $150-300.

stave in position to dress

Add $25 for the two-legged stand the jointer is set on.

HOWEL or CHIV

    right, $40-80.

CROZE

    left, $30-60.

Note: The look of a tool sometimes adds great value. A 19th century Austrian 3-arm cooper's croze with elaborate carvings brought $7035 in a 1997 English auction.

SUN PLANE, LEVELING PLANE, or TOPPING PLANE

beech, $45-85.

apple, $65-100.

lignum, $85-125.

COMBINATION COOPER'S PLANE

A combination of howel, croze, or sun plane, $75-175.

ROUTER

These tools are almost always craftsman-made, reflecting individual artistry, design, and workmanship. The more sculptured pieces run to the high end of the price range. Some, with ornate carvings or made of exotic woods and inlays, are worth from $150 to $400.

"D" style, granny tooth, wedged iron,
   left, $30-75.

"D" style, granny tooth, thumbscrewed iron,
   top right and bottom, $40-100.

Plain, solid body granny tooth,
   $20-40.

COACHMAKER'S ROUTER

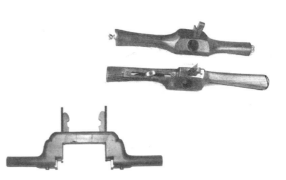

Boxing router, *top,* $20-50.

Fenced router, *bottom,* $30-75.

Double pistol grip router, $100-200.

Single pistol grip router, $100-200.
   The single router is worth approximately 25% more
   each if it comes with its matching piece to form a left
   and right pair.

COACHMAKER'S PLOW

Adjustable metal fence, *top,* $1000-2000.
   A superb rare Falconer coach plow sold for $22,500 at a 1998 auction.

Fixed fence, *center,* $400-800.
   The fixed fence coach plow is worth about 50% more each if it is sold
   with its matching piece to form a left and right pair.

Adjustable wood fence, *bottom,* $400-1500 (based on ornateness).

*A magnificent rosewood and brass coach plow, with a hinged
adjustable fence, sold for $4098 at a 2000 auction.*

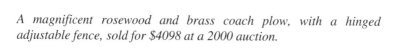

COACHMAKER'S T-RABBET

Flat sole, *left,* $20-40.

Convex sole, *right,* $25-45.

COACHMAKER'S MOLDING PLANE

The prices below are for beech. Add 50-100%
for boxwood or any other exotic wood.

Squirrel-tailed, *all shown,* $30-60.

Rectangular-shaped, $20-40.

Miniature, under 6", any shape. Generally the
smaller the plane, the greater the value. $30-60.

SPILL PLANE

Standard, $40-80.

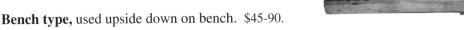

Bench type, used upside down on bench. $45-90.

ROUNDING PLANE or WITCHET

Fixed size, *top,* $45-90.

Adjustable size, *bottom,* $85-165.

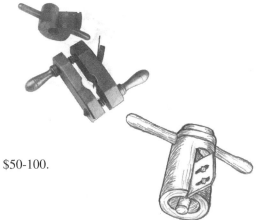

Turk's Head, for tapering ends of pipe logs, $50-100.

SHAVE

Hand shave (also called spokeshave), beech.

Add 50-100% for boxwood
straight iron sole, *top,* $8-18.
straight brass sole, *middle,* $12-25.
curved iron sole, $12-25.
curved brass sole, *bottom,* $15-30.
over 12" x 2", $25-50.
adjustable blade, $20-40.

Cooper's shave
inshave, *left,* $30-60.
plucker, *right,* $60-120.

head swift or head float, iron 3" or over, *left,* $40-80.
downright, iron under 3", *right,* $35-65.

Jarvis, concave sole, *top left,* $45-90.

Nelson, flat sole, *top right,* $40-80.

Handrail shave
double, *bottom,* $50-100.
single, $35-70.

BEADER

Windsor patent
walnut, $150-225.
ebonized, $100-200.

PATTERNMAKER'S PLANE

This plane has 5-10 replaceable soles with their
corresponding contoured blades, usually simple
concave and convex,
smoother, *right,* $75-150.
jack, $90-175.

SCRAPER

Owner-made, *top*, $12-30.

Factory-made
laminated, *bottom,* $60-120.
solid (similar to above), $35-70.

CONTINENTAL EUROPEAN PLANES

HORNED or BISMARCK   (Generally German or Austrian.)

Chip carved, *bottom,* $60-150.

Standard (without any carving), $20-40.

Iron cap with thumbscrew, *top,* $30-60.

FRENCH PLANE

These planes are generally made of cormier wood, which has the appearance of applewood.

Single iron, molding, *top left,* $20-50.

Double iron, molding, *top right,* $35-80.

Decorative plow, *bottom left,* $75-150.

Plow, *bottom right,* $60-120.

DUTCH PLANE

Jack (roffel), *top left,* $100-225.
> *A jack plane dated 1729 sold at auction for $3260.*

Block smoother (blockschaaf), carved and dated, *top center,* $600-1200.
> Earlier dates (prior to ca. 1760) command higher prices.

Rabbet (boorschaaf), *top right,* $25-50.

Scroll smoother (gerfschaaf), *bottom left,* $50-100.
> In some American descriptions this is referred to as a schaaf plane.

Plow (ploeg), *bottom center*, $100-225.
> dated in 1700s, $750-1500.

ASIATIC PLANE

Indonesian carved jack plane

(Note: wedge and iron are missing in the example shown), top.
> $150-300 with wedge and iron complete.

Chinese smoothing plane, *bottom,* $40-80.

SECTION 2

American Wooden Planes With a Planemaker's or Dealer's Imprint

Over 400 makers are shown in the **Planemaker's Directory** that follows. Though only a fraction of those that are known, they encompass many of the most important as well as the most prolific American planemakers and dealers.

If a planemaker has more than one imprint, and there is a significant value difference between them, it will be denoted with an asterisk after the maker's name. In all cases, only the most common of that maker's imprints will be used to determine the Value Number. For further information regarding makers, see *A Guide to the Makers of American Wooden Planes.* (see Bibliography).

The condition of the imprint will affect the value of the plane, and the effect can vary considerably. A rare 18th century plane having a crisp full imprint might be worth *up to 100%* more than the same plane with a faint imprint.

On the other hand, in the case of common 19th century imprints, the condition of the imprint changes the value very little, probably in the range of 5% - 10%. As for illegible imprints, they are considered to be in the same category as unmarked planes, and are priced as in Section 1 of this chapter.

HOW TO FIND THE VALUE OF YOUR IMPRINTED PLANE

1. Find the planemaker's imprint on your plane. It is almost always found on the toe (front) of the plane. See page 29 for hints to distinguish maker marks from owner marks.

2. Look up the planemaker's name in the **Planemaker's Directory**, pgs. 47-51. Next to the name of each planemaker will be a Value Number (1 through 10). This number represents the comparative value of that maker's most common imprints, 10 being the most valuable.

3. Look down the left hand column of the **Value Chart**, pgs. 52-53, listing the different types of planes, until you find your plane's type, and then look horizontally across the line until you reach the column that has the same Value Number heading that you found above. There you will find the estimated value of your plane in GOOD to GOOD PLUS condition. To adjust the value for a condition other than GOOD to GOOD PLUS, refer back to the Introduction.

PLANEMAKER'S DIRECTORY

* = significantly rarer marks exist. See previous page.

A. Adams 7

T. Aikman 4

Alford 4

C. Allen * 4

D. Amsden 4

Andruss 1

J. Andruss 3

O. Andrus 2

J. or J.J. Angermyer 5

Thos. L. Appleton 1

B. Armitage 8

William Armstrong 4

Arnold & Crouch 1

Arnold & Field 6

Arrowmammett 1

Atkinson 3

T. Atkinson 2

Auburn Tool Co. 1

Adam Ault 5

Samuel Auxer 5

Auxer & Remley 6

J.R. Bachelder 3

R.C. Bailey 3

A. & E. Baldwin * 1

E. Baldwin 2

Ion Ballou 9

Jno. M. Barkley 4

A. Barnes * 1

R. Barnes 2

S.S. Barry 2

Barry & Co. 3

Barry & Way 1

A.C. Bartlett's Ohio Planes 1

D.R. Barton & Co. 1

Barton & Smith 2

E. Bassett 6

Iohn Bassett 8

J.E. Bassett & Co. 2

J.F. Bauder * 5

E.Z. Baxter 7

Beacher & Addis 3

Israel O. Beattie * 2

W.B. Belch * 2

John Bell 2

Benson & Crannell 1

Bensen & M'Call 2

Bensen & Munsell 2

Bensen & Parry 2

David Benson 1

Benson & Mockridge 2

G.A. Benton 2

Benton, Evans & Co. 3

B.F. Berry 2

E. Berry 4

Bewley 2

S.H. Bibighaus 2

Biddle & Co. 2

R. & W.C. Biddle & Co. 2

A.F. or G.L. Bidwell 2

L.B. Bigelow 3

Bigelow & Barrus 4

L. Biglow 4

C. Blasdell 5

I. Blossom 7

Bodman & Hussey 2

Boston Factory 3

J. Bradford 2

S. Branch 6

G. Bremerman 2

E. Briggs 9

N. Briggs 7

P. Brooks or P. Brooks & Co.* 1

W. Brooks * 5

J.T. Brown 3

Brumley 5

T.E. Burley 7

Geo. Burnham, Jr. 1

Burn ham, Fox & Co. 2

Bush 3

Butler * 3

E.W. Carpenter * 4

I. or S. or W. Carpenter 6

Edward Carter 1

E. & C. Carter 1

R. Carter 1

R. & C. or R. & L.
    Carter 1

S. Caruthers 7

L. Case 1

Casey & Co. 1

Casey, Clark & Co. 1

Casey, Kitchel & Co. 1

H. Chapin 1

N. Chapin & Co. 1

Chapin-Stephens 1

P. Chapin * 2

J. Chappell 4

C., J., or S. Chase 6

Ce. Chelor * 10

J.E. Child 1

Child, Pratt & Co. 1

E. Clark 7

E. Clifford 7

J. Coates 4

R.J. Collins 4

D. Colton 2

D. Colton & J. Colton 2

D. Colton & B. Sheneman 2

J. Colton 2

Conway Tool Co. 2

S. Cook 3

S.C. Cook * 2

D. Copeland 1

D. & M. Copeland 1

M. Copeland * 1

M. & A. Copeland * 1

Copeland & Co. 1

J. Coughtry 4

D.O. Crane * 2

M. Crannell 1

J. Creagh 2

W. Cuddy 2

A. Cumings * 2

S. Cumings * 3

F. Dallicker 4

E. Danberry 2

B. Dean 6

S. Dean 8

L. DeForest 1

G.W. Denison & Co. 1

J. Denison * 1

M. Deter 6

S. Doggett * 7

J. Donaldson 2

T. Donoho 4

Marten Doscher 1

S.C. Dunham &
    T.J. M'Master 3

Charles Dupee 9

A.R. Earl 2

Eastburn or
    R. Eastburn * 3

Easterly & Co. 2

Eayrs & Co. 2

Empire Tool Co. 1

W.L. Epperson 3

E. & J. Evans 1

J.W. Farr & Co. * 1

S.E. Farrand 2

Isaac Field 3

Field & Hardie 2

A. Fish 2

C. or J. or N. Fisher 6

Abraham Fisk 6

L. Fox & Son 2

Fox & Washburn 2

John Frace 3

G. Freburger, Jr. 5

C. Fuller * 2

D. Fuller * 3

Jo. Fuller * 5

Fuller & Field 5

L. Gardner 1

Gardner & Brazer 3

Gardner & Murdock 2

Genesee Tool * 1

C.M. Gere 3

E. Gere * 4

N. Gere 5

J.W. Gibbs 3

Gibbs & Cation 3

J. Gibson 1

P.A. Gladwin & Co. * 1

Gladwin & Appleton 1

T. Goldsmith * 3

Wm. Goldsmith 3

Jn. Gordon 4

F.J. Gouch 1

Gouch & Demond 2

Tho. Grant * 4

Greenfield Tool Co. 1

W. Grinel 4

Hall, Case & Co. 1

A. Hammacher & Co. 2

Hammacher, Schlemmer &
    Co. * 2

L.S. Hapgood 3

J.W. Harron * 1

R. Harron 1

C. Harwood 4

P. Hayden & Co. 2

Addison Heald 2

D. Heis or D. Heiss 5

Iacob Heiss 4

R.W. Hendrickson * 2

A. Hide 8

H. Hills 1

Hills & Winship 2

R. Hoey 3

C.W. Holden 2

A. Howland & Co. * 1

W.S. Howland 2

Hull & Montgomery 3

Hunt & Wiseman 1

A. Inglis * 3

I. Iones 9

R. Ionson 6

H.L. James 1

J.T. Jones * 2

I. Jones - see I. Iones

R.Jonson - see R. Ionson

J. Kellogg * 1

A. Kelly & Co. 1

H.L. Kendall * 2

Kennedy or L. Kennedy * 3

Kennedy & White 2

Kennedy, Barry & Way 2

Kieffer & Auxer 5

J. Killam * 2

J.A. King 8

Josiah or J. King * 1

Kneass or Kneass & Co. 3

Laird 4

W.G. or J.H. Lamb 1

Lamb & Brownell 2

F. Lender 2

Lindenberger 4

C. Lindenberger 3

I. Lindenberger 5

J.F. & G.M. Lindsey 1

L. Little * 4

N. Little 4

Wm. H. Livingston & Co. 2

D. Long 3

I. Long 4

M. Long 3

Lyon & Smith 2

T.J. M'Master & Co. * 2

Z.J. M'Master & Co. * 2

R.W. Maccubbin 2

F.B. Marble 2

Marley 3

Martin or W. Martin * 5

J.W. Massey 4

A. Meier & Co. 2

A. Mockridge 2

Mockridge & Francis 1

Mockridge & Son 2

Montgomery 3

Montgomery &
    Woodbridge 2

A.G. Moore 1

B. Morrill 2

E. Moses * 4

T. or Thos. Napier * 6

H.L. Narramore 2

E. Newell 5

New York Tool Co. 1

F. Nicholson * 10

I. Nicholson 9

H. or S. Niles 7

B. Norman 5

N. Norton 4

S. Noyes 5

E., E.P., J.H., or
    N. Nutting 4

Ogontz Tool Co. * 1

Ohio Tool Co. * 1

J. or W. Oothoudt 3

Owasco Tool Co. * 1

Parker, Hubbard
    & Co. * 1

J. or C. Parkhurst 4

Geo. Parr 1

Parrish 6

R.A. Parrish * 3

John Passcul 7

J. Pearce 1

J.W. Pearce * 2

E.W. Pennell 3

Pennell & Miller 3

Phoenix Company 2

E. Pierce 5

1. Pike 8

S. Pomeroy 6

W.H. Pond 1

N. Potter 9

Pratt & Co. 1

D. Presbrey 4

S. Presbrey 6

P. Probasco 3

P. Quigley 3

S. Randall 2

Randall & Bensen 2

Randall & Cook 2

W. Raymond * 4

Reed * 1

Reed & Auerbacher 2

Richards 7

Rickard 4

P.B. Rider 3

E.C. Ring 1

E. & T. Ring & Co. 1

G. & W.H. Roseboom 2

Wm. C. Ross 3

S. Rowell * 2

E. Safford 3

A. Sampson 3

L. Sampson 6

D.P. Sanborn * 1

Sanborn & Gouch 2

Sandusky Tool Co. * 1

D. Sargent 1

P. Sargent 2

Sargent & Co. 1

1. Schauer 4

N. Schauer 5

H. Schmitt 2

Scioto Works 1

L. Scovill or L. Scovil * 3

J. Scovill 2

J. Searing 2

C.S. See 3

A.B. Seidensticker 3

E.F. Seybold * 1

Shapleigh, Day & Co. 1

B. Sheneman * 2

B. Sheneman & Bro. 2

Shiverick * 2

Shiverick & Malcolm 2

Arad:Simons 6

I. Sleeper 4

S. Sleeper 5

A. Smith 5

E. Smith * 2

W.M. Souder * 3

N. or W.H. Spaulding 2

John E. Spayd 5

Spayd & Bell 4

A.C. Spicer 5

O. Spicer 5

I. Stall 6

J. Stamm 3

W. Steele 3

A.C. Stevens 5

J. Stiles
    dated before 1800 7
    dated after 1800 5
    undated 3

H.G. Stilley
    exotic woods 7

J.P. Storer
    beech 3
    exotic woods 6

M. Stout 2

J.J. Styles 2

J.M. Taber 1

N. Taber 5

Wing H. Taber * 2

Taber Plane Co. 1

E. Taft 9

J.C. Taylor 2

R.M. Tilburn 3

T. Tileston 2

L. Tinkham 6

Joseph Titcomb 4

C. Tobey 5

J.R. Tolman 3

T.J. Tolman * 2

Jn. Tower 6

Tucker & Appleton 2

Union Factory — see
   H. Chapin

Union Tool Co. 2

Van Baun 4

W. Vance * 3

John Veit 2

J. or J.J. Vinall 2

I. or B. Walton or
   I:B: Waltons * 8

W.J.C. Ward 4

Ward & Fletcher 3

C. Warren * 2

W.L. Washburn 2

Way & Sherman 2

J. Webb 2

W. Webb * 4

Wm. P. Webb 5

J. Weeden 5

H. Wells * 1

R. Wells * 2

H. Wetherel 8

H. Wetherell * 4

A. Wheaton 6

G. White * 3

Henry G. White * 2

Israel White * 3

L. & I.J. White 2

Jo. Wilbur 8

A.J. Wilkinson & Co. 1

Winsted Plane Co. * 1

Woodruff & McBride 2

R. Wright 6

Young & M'Master * 2

VALUE CHART — Page 1

Priced from GOOD to GOOD+

	1	2	3	4	5
SMOOTHER	$ 7-15	12-25	20-40	35-75	65-130
JACK	12-22	15-30	25-50	40-80	70-140
FORE	15-25	20-40	35-70	60-100	80-160
JOINTER	20-30	25-50	40-80	70-120	90-180
RABBET	7-12	10-20	18-35	30-60	50-100
HOLLOW or ROUND	8-15	12-25	20-40	35-70	60-120
BEAD	10-20	15-30	25-50	40-80	70-140
DADO	15-30	20-40	35-70	60-100	80-160
TONGUE or GROOVE NO HDL.	12-22	15-30	25-50	40-80	65-130
TONGUE or GROOVE HDL.	18-30	25-50	30-60	50-100	80-160
COMBINATION T & G	30-50	40-75	65-120	100-175	150-250
PLANK, SLIDE ARM, HDL.	30-50	40-75	65-120	100-175	150-250
PLANK, SCREW ARM HDL.	35-60	50-90	80-150	125-250	175-300
MOVING FILLETSTER	25-50	40-70	50-100	85-175	150-250
SASH, SOLID	25-50	40-75	65-120	100-200	175-300
SASH, ADJUSTABLE	30-60	50-85	75-140	125-225	200-350
SASH, SCREW ARM	50-85	75-125	90-175	150-300	250-450
*SIMPLE MOLDER, UNDER 1¼"	18-40	30-50	40-70	60-120	100-200
*SIMPLE MOLDER, 1¼" & OVER	25-60	40-75	60-120	100-200	175-350
COMPLEX MOLDER, UNDER 1¼"	30-70	50-85	70-135	125-250	200-400
COMPLEX MOLDER, 1¼-1¾"	40-85	65-120	100-175	150-300	250-500
COMPLEX MOLDER, OVER 1¾"	60-135	100-200	175-300	250-500	400-800
PLOW - NO HANDLE:					
SLIDE ARM, BEECH	50-90	70-140	100-200	175-350	300-600
SCREW ARM, BEECH	75-150	100-200	150-300	250-500	400-800
APPLE or BOXWOOD	135-225	175-250	200-400	350-600	500-1000
ROSEWOOD	200-325	250-375	300-500	400-800	600-1200
EBONY	450-800	550-900	700-1200	1000-1800	1500-2500
PLOW - HANDLED:					
SCREW ARM, BEECH	90-175	125-200	175-350	300-600	500-1000
APPLE or BOXWOOD	175-325	275-400	350-600	425-800	600-1200
ROSEWOOD	300-500	400-600	500-800	600-1000	800-1500
EBONY	600-1000	800-1200	1000-1500	1200-2000	1800-3000
PANEL RAISER - NO ARMS	100-175	150-250	200-350	300-500	400-800
PANEL RAISER - WITH ARMS	150-275	200-350	300-500	400-800	600-1200
MOLDER/CROWN HANDLED					
2"	100-175	125-200	150-250	200-350	300-600
2½"	125-225	175-275	200-350	300-500	400-800
3"	175-300	225-325	275-425	350-600	500-900
4"	275-400	300-450	400-550	450-700	600-1000

* A simple molder e.g., plain astragal, ovolo, cove, ogee.   Dimensions shown are iron width.

VALUE CHART — Page 2

Priced from GOOD to GOOD+

	6	7	8	9	10
SMOOTHER	$ 125-250	225-450	400-800	600-1200	1000-2000
JACK	130-250	225-450	400-800	600-1200	1000-2000
FORE	135-250	225-450	400-800	600-1200	1000-2000
JOINTER	140-250	225-450	400-800	600-1200	1000-2000
RABBET	80-175	160-350	325-700	600-1200	1000-2000
HOLLOW or ROUND	90-180	170-350	325-700	600-1200	1000-2000
BEAD	100-200	180-350	325-700	600-1200	1000-2000
DADO	125-250	225-400	350-700	600-1200	1000-2000
TONGUE or GROOVE NO HDL.	100-200	180-350	325-700	600-1200	1000-2000
TONGUE or GROOVE HDL.	125-250	225-450	400-800	-	-
COMBINATION T & G, NO HDL.	200-400	350-700	600-1200	-	-
PLANK, SLIDE ARM, HDL.	200-400	350-700	600-1200	-	-
PLANK, SCREW ARM HDL.	250-450	-	-	-	-
MOVING FILLETSTER	200-400	350-700	600-1200	1000-2000	-
SASH, SOLID	250-450	400-800	700-1400	1200-2500	2000-3500
SASH, ADJUSTABLE	300-550	-	-	-	-
SASH, SCREW ARM	375-700	-	-	-	-
*SIMPLE MOLDER, UNDER 1¼"	175-350	325-650	600-1200	1000-2000	1500-2500
*SIMPLE MOLDER, 1¼" & OVER	300-600	500-1000	800-1500	1200-2500	2000-3500
COMPLEX MOLDER, UNDER 1¼"	350-700	600-1200	1000-1800	1500-3000	2500-4000
COMPLEX MOLDER, 1¼"-1¾"	450-900	800-1500	1200-2000	1800-3500	3000-5000
COMPLEX MOLDER, OVER 1¾"	700-1400	1200-2000	-	-	-
PLOW - NO HANDLE:					
SLIDE ARM, BEECH	500-1000	800-1500	1200-2000	1800-3500	3000-5000
SCREW ARM, BEECH	600-1200	-	-	-	-
APPLE or BOXWOOD	800-1500	-	-	-	-
ROSEWOOD	-	-	-	-	-
EBONY	-	-	-	-	-
PLOW - HANDLED:					
SCREW ARM, BEECH	800-1500	-	-	-	-
APPLE or BOXWOOD	1000-2000	-	-	-	-
ROSEWOOD	-	-	-	-	-
EBONY	-	-	-	-	-
PANEL RAISER - NO ARMS	600-1000	800-1500	1200-2000	1800-3500	3000-5000
PANEL RAISER - WITH ARMS	1000-2000	-	-	-	-
MOLDER/CROWN HANDLED					
2"	500-1000	800-1500	1200-2500	2000-4000	3500-6000
2½"	600-1200	1000-2000	1800-3500	3000-5500	4500-7500
3"	700-1400	1200-2500	2000-4000	3500-6500	5000-9000
4"	800-1600	1500-3000	2500-5000	4000-8500	-

* A simple molder e.g., plain astragal, ovolo, cove, ogee.   Dimensions shown are iron width.

WOOD-BOTTOMED PLANES

Priced from GOOD to GOOD+

The detailed conditions that were outlined for wooden planes also apply to wood-bottomed planes. The following comments relate to the metal parts not found on wooden planes, e.g., the frame, cap, frog, and the plane iron adjustment parts. For these to be considered GOOD they must:

1. Retain at least half of their original japanning or plating. *Properly* replated or rejapanned parts are acceptable for GOOD.

2. Have solid castings. Cracks and discernable weld repairs are not acceptable for GOOD.

3. Have no chips or breakaways in the casting greater than ¼" in any direction, and these defects must not detract from function.

The Stanley line of wood-bottomed bench planes included 23 models, ranging from a 7" smoother to a 30" jointer. Although these planes were produced in the millions from 1869 to 1943, the early types are uncommon and sell for substantially more than the common types. As was said in the Introduction, the pricing shown in this Guide is based on the most common model, i.e., the one that was most produced and therefore most likely to be found today.

For those who wish to pursue the subject of model varieties including the rarities, or to learn more about wood-bottomed planes, we recommend *Patented Transitional & Metallic Planes in America 1827-1927* by Roger K. Smith, and *Antique & Collectible Stanley Tools* by John Walter, (see Bibliography).

In almost all cases of Stanley wood-bottomed planes, the number of the plane is shown on the nose.

BENCH PLANE

Stanley #21 smoother 7" (similar to #24),
$100-225.

Stanley #24 smoother 8", *right*, $25-50.

Stanley #25 block (similar to #24), $175-300.

Stanley #27 jack, *right*, $20-40.
Stanley #29 fore (similar to #27), $25-50.
Stanley #32 jointer (similar to #27), $30-60.

Stanley #35 or #36 smoother 9" or 10", $20-40.

Stanley Gage #G22 smoother 10", $45-90.

Stanley Gage #G26 jack 14", $45-90.

Stanley Gage #G30 jointer 22" (similar to #G26),
   $50-100.

To celebrate the 1876 national centennial, Stanley produced a line of planes with a **Liberty Bell** an
a "**76**" cast into the cap. The wood-bottomed models were:

Stanley #122 smoother, $25-50.

Stanley #127 jack, $25-50.

Stanley #129 fore (similar to #127), $30-60.
Stanley #132 jointer (similar to #127), $35-70.

Stanley #135 smoother, $30-60.

Some of the better known companies, besides Stanley, that sold wood-bottomed planes are shown below. The most common models are priced and can be used as a point of reference. They have the same general appearance as Stanley and usually have their company name on the nose and/or on the cutting iron.

Birmingham jack, $25-50.

Chaplin jack, $35-70.

Keen Kutter jack, $25-50.

Ohio jack, $20-40.

Multiform Moulding Co. (Worall's patent)
    jointer plane
        iron plate on top of entire body, *right,*
            $200-300.
        without iron plate, $100-200.
    match plane or molding plane with a removeable handle,
        complete with handle, $250-500.
        without handle, $35-75.

Sargent jack, $20-40.

Siegley jack, $25-50.

Standard Rule jack, $60-125.

Union jack, $20-40.

Upson Nut Co. jack, $20-40.

Winchester jack, $60-125.

AMERICAN METAL PLANES

Priced from GOOD to GOOD+

In this section there is considerable concentration on Stanley-made planes. This is because Stanley was the predominant American (and world) metal plane manufacturer. Also listed are many of the non-Stanley manufacturers that the reader might come across at auctions or on dealers' tables.

The coverage of American metal planes, while hardly exhaustive, includes the majority of the material usually seen. Pricing is based upon the condition GOOD to GOOD PLUS, **using the common model** of any particular plane. The criteria for these conditions are the same as was previously used for wood-bottomed planes. Some tools in their original boxes (mostly Stanley) are worth double (or more) their price without the box. Light rust and minor pitting are allowed for GOOD.

SOME METAL PLANE COMPANIES

The examples shown on the following five pages are mostly jack planes, generally the most common of the plane types. Non-Stanley smooth planes are usually worth considerably more than their jack cousins. Coverage has been expanded in the case of Sargent & Co. which, like Stanley, was an important manufacturer and about whom there is increasing collector interest. Information on other companies and models can be found in the Bibliography.

Bayley core box, *right,* $175-300.

Birmingham

    block plane, many models, $50-150.

    wood handle and knob, "B"-plane jack
       (similar to Stanley), $25-50.

    cast iron handle and knob, jack, $175-350.

    cast iron handle and knob, T-rabbet, $225-450.

Boston Metallic pierced sole smoother, $225-450.

Brown's Toboggan plane, $125-200.

Challenge (Tower and Lyon Co.) fore plane,
$600-1200.

Chaplin's patent (Tower and Lyon Co.) jack,
$50-100.

Defiance (Bailey Tool Co.) smoother,
"Battle Axe" logo on blade, $250-425.

Franklin shoe block plane, $75-125.

Hahn smoother, $65-135.

Holly's patent smoother, $750-1500.
(Example in photo has front knob added.)

Keen Kutter #K5 jack (similar to Stanley), $35-70.

Knowles' patent smoother, *right*, $750-1500.

Knowles'-type jack, $200-400 (based on similarity to original).
Note: The subtle difference between the original Knowles' patent (the first American patented iron plane) and the subsequent look-alikes, called Knowles'-type, can be found in Patented Transitional & Metallic Planes in America 1827-1927.

Metallic Plane Co. fore plane
single adjusting lever, *right,* $85-175.
no adjusting lever (similar to above), $100-200.

star wheel adjusting knob, *right,* $125-225.

three adjusting levers, ogee handle tip, $150-275.

Morris patent jack, $750-1500.

Ohio Tool Co. #05 jack (similar to Stanley), $20-45.

Rodier's patent jointer, $600-1200.

Sargent & Co.

#34 dado, $100-200.

#43 scraper, $75-150.

#59 scraper, $125-225.

#74 circular, $125-225.

#79 filletster and rabbet,
$25-50.

#81 side rabbet, $75-150.

#160 scrub,
    wood knob & handle, $100-200.
    iron knob & handle, $125-225.

One of the rarest Sargent planes, the double-bladed #162 scrub, sold in a 1997 auction for $3000, and in a 1999 auction for $3400.

#196 rabbet, $35-75.

#408 smoother (similar to Stanley #3), $25-45.

#414 jack, $20-40.

#422 jointer (similar to #414), $35-50.

#507 carriage block plane, $100-200.

#514 low angle jack, $250-450.

#708 autoset smoother (similar to #714), $60-120.

#714 autoset jack, $60-120.

#722 autoset jointer, tilt knob, $100-200.
    (similar to #714).

#1080 combination plane with cutters and
    pasteboard box, $100-200.

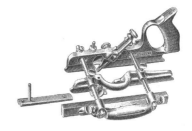

#1085 combination plane with cutters and "suitcase" case, $300-500.

#1506 cabinetmaker's rabbet ("ladybug"), $300-500.

Larger sizes and models with fences range up to $2500 in G+ condition. (See Dave Heckel's *Sargent Value Guide*)

#5307 low angle knuckle cap block plane, $18-35.

Shelton smoother, $12-20.

Siegley fore plane, $40-80.

Standard Rule Co. jack, $125-250.

Stanley jack

#5 (see page 63).

#605 Bedrock, $85-150.
Flat-topped sides are later than round-topped sides. Differences in price between the two styles are not consistent. (See John Walter's book.)

#G-5 Gage, $100-200.

Steer's patent (Brattleboro Tool Co.) jack, $175-350.

Union

#5 jack (similar to Stanley), $20-40.

#X4 smoother, *right,* $30-60.

A Union #0 (size of the Stanley #1) sold for $6250 at a 2000 auction.

Victor (Leonard Bailey & Co.) #5 jack
metal handle and decorative knob, $250-400.

Winchester W5 jack (similar to Stanley), $70-135.

STANLEY "CLASSICS"   (just a few)

The planes listed below are priced as complete, with all accessories and blades, *without* their boxes.

Stanley #42 Miller's patent gunmetal plow, $1800-2800.

Stanley #A45 aluminum combination plow
(similar to #45), $1750-2500.

Stanley #56 corebox plane, $800-1600.

Stanley #64 butcher block plane, $900-1800.

Stanley #87 scraper plane, $1000-2000.

Stanley #101½ block plane, $450-650.

Stanley #164 low angle plane, $2000-4000.

Stanley #196 curve rabbet plane, $1200-2200.

Stanley #212 scraper plane, $800-1500.

In a 2000 auction, a #212 in FINE condition, in the original box, sold for $3600.

Stanley #340 furring plane, $1000-1800.

Stanley #444 dovetail plane, $800-1250.

Note: As the original box is almost always available with the dovetail plane, it is included in the price above.

Miller's patent 1872 plow plane

   cast iron $8000-12,000.
   bronze $14,000-20,000.

In a 1999 international auction, a bronze model in FINE condition sold for $23,500.

BENCH PLANE

Stanley #1 smoother 5½" long (number not shown on plane), *bottom*, $850-1250.

Stanley #2 smoother (similar to #3), $225-275.

Stanley #3 smoother, *second from bottom*, $40-80.

Stanley #4 smoother (similar to #3), $20-45.

Stanley #4½ smoother (similar to #3), $50-100.

Stanley #5 jack, *second from top*, $20-45.

Stanley #5¼ jack (similar to #5), $40-80.

Stanley #5½ jack (similar to #5), $45-90.

Stanley #6 fore (similar to #5), $30-60.

Stanley #7 jointer (similar to #8), $45-100.

Stanley #8 jointer, *top,* $60-120.

All of the bench planes above, except the #1, also came with corrugated soles and were designated by the suffix "C" after the model number. They are worth only slightly more than the standard flat soles, except in the cases of the 2C and the 5¼C, which are worth $300-500 and $175-275 respectively.

As with almost all tools (or antiques in general), the earlier models are worth more than the later ones. For further details of this differentiation see *Patented Transitional & Metallic Planes in America 1827-1927* and John Walter's *Antique & Collectible Stanley Tools*. An early model #3 (a vertical post Bailey) sold for $4500 in a 1997 auction, and another sold for $5700 in a 2000 auction.

Three characteristics that can be helpful in determining the model age are:

The front knob is 2" or less in height on the earlier models. Later models have knobs over 2".

The name "Stanley" on the lever cap is absent on the earlier models.

The lateral adjusting lever (behind the blade) is absent on the very early models. These are called pre-laterals and can be worth considerably more than those with adjusting levers (see John Walter's book).

Note: When checking for the lateral adjusting lever, make sure it is not broken off.

Along with the wood-bottomed bench planes in the Liberty Bell series, Stanley also produced two metal-bodied planes that carried the Liberty Bell cap:

Stanley #104 smoother, *right*, $100-225.

Stanley #105 jack (similar to #104), $100-225.

Stanley also produced aluminum-bodied planes (the model numbers are preceded with the letter A) in addition to steel-bodied planes (the model numbers are preceded with the letter S). The aluminum models are similar to the standard cast iron models. Some of these are:

Stanley #A4 smoother (similar to #4), $100-200.

Stanley #A5 jack (similar to #5), $100-200.

Stanley #S4 smoother (similar to the S5 below), $100-200.

Stanley #S5 jack, $100-200.

SCRAPER

Stanley #12 veneer scraper (similar to the 12½ next page), $50-100.

Stanley #12¼ veneer scraper (similar to the 12½, next page), $200-300.

C

Stanley #12½ veneer scraper, *C-top left,*
  $60-125.

Stanley #70 box scraper, $12-30 .

Stanley #80 cabinet scraper, *C-bottom,* $15-35.

Stanley #81 cabinet scraper, $40-80.

Stanley #83 cabinet scraper, adjustable roller guide,
  $50-100.

Stanley #85 cabinetmaker's scraper plane,
  $550-750.

Stanley #112 cabinet scraper plane, *C-top right,*
  $135-225.

Boufford patent hand scraper, $150-300.

Eclipse scraper, $350-600.

CIRCULAR PLANE

Stanley #13 circular plane, 10½" (number not shown
  on plane), $90-150.

Stanley #20 circular plane, $80-135.

Stanley #113 circular plane, $90-150.

Evans' patent circular plane, $100-175.
with brass tag, $200-350.

BLOCK PLANE

Stanley #9 cabinetmaker's block plane (number not shown on plane), $800-1200.

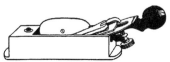

Although a side handle ("hot dog") was provided for these planes, it rarely is found with them. The price above excludes these handles. Should one be present, add $400-600. This plane is susceptible to cracks in the casting, particularly in the rear body where the handle is attached. The cracks may only be hairline, or they may even be weld repaired, but in either case they will reduce the condition of the plane to GOOD MINUS. *Condition, condition, condition! A #9 in superb condition with the original "hotdog" went for $4239 at a 1997 auction. One in near perfect condition, without the hotdog and in the original box, sold for $8000 at a 2000 auction!*

Stanley #9½ block (number not shown on plane), 6" long, $12-25.

Stanley #9¾ block (number not shown on plane). Identical to the 9½, except for a removeable rear handle with rosewood knob. $225-325.

Stanley #15 block (number not shown on plane). (Similar to #9½, except 7".) $12-25.

Stanley #15½ block (number not shown on plane). Identical to the #15, except for a removeable rear handle with rosewood knob. $225-325.
At a 2000 auction, a FINE #15½, in the original box, sold for $2500.

Stanley #18 block (number not shown on plane),
"Knuckle" cap, $20-35.

Stanley #60½ low angle block (number stamped on side),
D-right, $25-45.

D

Stanley #110 block, $6-12.

Stanley #120 block, *D-left,* $8-15.

Stanley #130 double end block, $35-70.

Stanley #140 rabbet and block, $90-150.
Watch for replaced screws in the side plate.

Stanley #220 block, $10-18.

DADO PLANE

Stanley #39 dado

$\frac{1}{4}$" or $\frac{3}{8}$" cutter, $75-150.

$\frac{1}{2}$" or $\frac{5}{8}$" cutter, $85-165.

$\frac{3}{4}$" or $\frac{7}{8}$" cutter, $100-185.

1" cutter, $125-200.

Stanley #239 special dado
⅛" cutter, $125-225, with cutters up to
½" cutter, $200-350.

PLOW and COMBINATION PLANE

A few early models were japanned and are valued much higher by collectors. However, users will pay more for the "improved" later models, which were nickel-plated. Most factory boxes for the Stanley #45 and #55 are quite common, but add slightly to the prices shown.

Stanley #41 adjustable plow, Miller's patent 1870, similar to Stanley #42, (p. 62) but cast iron.
complete with filletster bed and all cutters, $800-1250.
1 cutter and filletster bed, $400-750.
1 cutter, no filletster bed, $175-350.

Stanley #43 adjustable plow, Miller's patent 1870. There should not be any holes in the skate, as the #43 did not take a filletster bed. Similar to Stanley #42, (p. 62) but cast iron, and without the filletster bed.
complete with all cutters, $350-600.
1 cutter only, $150-250.

Stanley #45 combination plane, *right*
complete, all accessories and cutters, $150-250.
1 cutter only, $45-90.

Stanley #46 skew cutter combination plane, similar to #45 but cutter is skewed.
complete, all accessories and cutters, $150-275.
1 cutter only, $50-125.

Stanley #50 light combination plane
complete, all accessories and cutters, $85-175.
1 cutter only, $30-50.

Stanley #55 universal combination plane

complete, all accessories and cutters, $300-500.
1 cutter only, $125-225.

Stanley #238 weatherstrip plow, $125-225.

Stanley #248 weatherstrip plow, $50-100.
#248A, with all 7 cutters. $70-150.

Siegley combination plane

complete, all cutters, $175-325.
1 cutter only, $75-150.

Phillips Plough

There are a variety of models, looking somewhat different from one another. Refer to *Patented Transitional & Metallic Planes in America 1827-1927* for details.

left, $600-1500

right, $1500-4000 depending upon degree of pinstriping and number of cutters.

Fales patent combination plane

Although 160 attachments and cutters make it complete, it is rarely found with more than 100 total pieces.
50-100 cutters and forms, $500-1000.
1 cutter only, $75-150.

Walker patent adjustable face plane

complete with all cutters, $600-1200.
one cutter only, $350-700.

Morris patent " scissors" adjustment fence
1 cutter, $2500-4500.
This plane sold, with the rare 9 cutters, for $6100 at a 2000 auction.

TONGUE and GROOVE PLANE or MATCH PLANE

Stanley #48 tongue and groove plane (similar to #49),
$50-100.

Stanley #49 tongue and groove plane, *at righ*t, $60-120.

Stanley #146 match plane (similar to #147), $125-250.

Stanley #147 match plane, *at right*, $125-250.

Stanley #148 match plane (similar to #147), $75-135.

ROUTER   (with only one cutter)

Stanley #71 router, *at right,* $30-50.

Stanley #71½ router (similar to #71), $30-50.

Stanley #171 door trim and router, $250-400.

Stanley #271 router, $20-35.

RABBET PLANE

Stanley #10 carriagemaker's rabbet, *at right,* $100-200.

Stanley #10½ carriagemaker's rabbet (similar
to #10), non-adj. mouth, $100-200.

Stanley #10¼ carriagemaker's rabbet (similar
to #10, but with tilt handles), $400-650.

Stanley #78 duplex plane, *E- top,* $35-60.
(must have fence and depth stop).   **E**

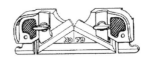

Stanley #79 side rabbet early type, $50-100.

Stanley #80 or #90 steel-cased rabbet, $100-250.

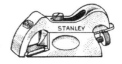

Stanley #90 bull nose rabbet, $50-100.
    (One of the rare cases where two Stanley tools in the same sub-group have the same model number, i.e., #90 rabbet planes).

Stanley #92 cabinetmaker's rabbet, *prev. pg.* **E**-*bottom*, $75-150.

Stanley #93 cabinetmaker's rabbet (similar to #92), $100-200.

Stanley #94 cabinetmaker's rabbet (similar to #92), $225-450.

Stanley #98 or #99 side rabbet, $50-100.
    (add 25% for a matched pair of #98 and #99).

Stanley #180, #181, or #182 rabbet, *prev. pg.* **E**-*center*, $35-60.

Stanley #190, #191, or #192 rabbet (similar to #180), $20-40.

Stanley #278 rabbet and filletster, $150-275.

Stanley #289 filletster and rabbet, $200-350.

Stanley #378 weatherstrip rabbet, $100-175.

T-rabbet with "squirrel tail" handle
   iron, $50-125.
   brass or bronze, $75-175.

MINIATURE

Stanley #75 bull nose rabbet, *left,* $20-35.

Stanley #100½ block, *center,* $75-125.

Stanley #101 block, *right,* $15-30.

Stanley #100 block, $20-40.

SHAVE   (also called spokeshave)

Stanley #51 or #52, $8-15.

Stanley #53 or #54, $10-20.

Stanley #60, *F-bottom left,* $25-50.

F

Stanley #63, convex bottom, $10-20.

Stanley #65, *F-top left*, $65-135.

Stanley #67
   2 bottoms, one fence, $75-150.
   1 bottom, no fence, $40-80.

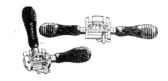

Stanley #84 or #85, $50-100.

Stanley #152, $15-30.

Millers Falls, *prev. pg. F-bottom right*, $30-60.

Patent "Gull Wing," *prev. pg. F-top right*, $30-60.

Stearns, with adjustable sole, *top,* $65-125.

Cincinnati Tool, *center,* $30-60.

Preston (English), *bottom,* $45-90.

All bronze or brass, $25-85
   (based on decorativeness.)

METAL BEADER

Stanley #66 hand beader
   All 8 cutters, 2 fences, $75-150.
   1 cutter, 1 fence, $40-70.

Stanley #69 hand beader, 6 cutters, $250-450.

SPECIAL FUNCTION PLANES

   These are some planes produced by Stanley that the reader might run across. They are somewhat unusual in their applications, but worthy of inclusion. Naturally all of these special planes could not be included.

Stanley #11 beltmaker's plane, $85-175.

Stanley #40 scrub plane, $45-90.

Stanley #52 shoot board & plane,
   right, $750-1200.

Stanley #51 shoot board plane only,
   $175-350.

Stanley #57 core box plane
>   with one set of extensions, $225-350.
>   with no extensions, $60-120.

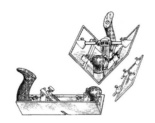

Stanley #62 low angle plane, $250-450.

Stanley #72 chamfer plane, $200-325.

Stanley #74 floor plane
>   with original handle, $600-900.
>   without handle, $150-300.

Stanley #95 edge trimming block plane, $85-125.

Stanley #96 chisel gauge plane, 2¼", $125-200.

Stanley #97 cabinetmaker's edge plane, $350-550.

Stanley #144 corner rounding plane, $200-325.

Stanley #193 fibre board cutter plane, fences,
> $60-120.

OTHER STANLEY SERIES

In the Stanley family of planes there are entire groups of generically similar models that Stanley either acquired from other companies or put out on its own. They are:

1. The Liberty Bell series
2. The Victor series
3. The Bed Rock series
4, The Gage series
5. The Four Square series
6. The Aluminum series
7. The Defiance series
8. The Two-Tone series
9. The Steel series

Some representative samples of most of these series are shown in this *Guide*. Complete pricing will be found in *Antique & Collectible Stanley Tools* by John Walter (see Bibliography).

"ENGLISH-STYLE" METAL PLANES

Planes similar to those shown in the following chapter (ENGLISH METAL PLANES), but made by American manufacturers are very collectible. Almost all of these makers are from New York City. They are: J. Popping, L. Brandt, G. Thorested, J. Erlandsen and N. Erlandsen.

Shoulder plane (rabbet planes with straight tops are slightly less in value)
cast iron or steel, $400-800.
bronze or brass, $700-1200.
A fancy bronze shoulder plane by J. Popping (in superb condition) sold for $5750 at a 2000 auction.

Bullnose plane
cast iron or steel, $250-400.
bronze or brass, $350-600.

Miter Plane
cast iron or steel, $1500-3000.

ENGLISH METAL PLANES

Priced from GOOD to GOOD+

Today's prices for some of the English and Scottish metal planes may prove surprising. Norris, Mathieson, and Spiers are the most sought after by both users and collectors, attracted by their outstanding quality, handsome appearance, and accuracy in use. In an English auction a unique model of a Norris A-11 adjustable miter plane sold for $8200. However others, depending upon rarity and condition, sell for several hundred up to several thousand dollars.

The prices shown below are for planes whose wooden parts are made of rosewood. The use of walnut or mahogany tends to put the value in the lower portion of the price range, while ebony raises it to the upper portion. The term "dovetailed" refers to the manner in which the sole of the plane is jointed to the sides.

Norris, Spiers, Mathieson, Preston, and Record planes are not averaged into the prices directly below, but are handled separately at the end of this section.

Note: A magnificent reproduction of a 26½" adjustable brass jointer sold for $5232 in 1997, proving that craftsmanship is still one of the important variables that determine value.

SMOOTH PLANE

Unhandled

 cast iron or steel, *right,* $100-225.

 steel, dovetailed, $125-275.

Handled

 cast iron or steel, $150-275.

 steel, dovetailed, $175-300.

 gunmetal or brass, $200-350.

 Scottish, ornate knob and/or side profile, *left above,* $250-500.

PANEL PLANE 13½" - 17½" (occasionally 12" or 12½")

Cast iron or steel, $200-325.

Steel, dovetailed, *at right,* $225-375.

Gunmetal or brass, $250-450.

JOINTER PLANE 18½" - 22½" (models longer than 22½" are rare)

Cast iron or steel (similar to panel plane above), $250-450.

Steel, dovetailed (similar to panel plane above), $300-500.

SHOULDER PLANE

Rebate (or rabbet) planes are similar to shoulder planes, but have straight, rather than contoured tops. Usually, they are slightly lower in price.

Cast iron or steel, $75-175.

Steel, dovetailed, *top*, $100-200.

Gunmetal or brass, $150-300.

BULL NOSE PLANE

Cast iron or steel, *above center,* $50-100.

Gunmetal or brass, $85-175.

CHARIOT PLANE

Cast iron or steel, *above bottom,* $75-150.

Gunmetal or brass, $100-200.

MITER PLANE

Cast iron or steel, $175-350.

Steel, dovetailed, *all at right*, $250-500.

Gunmetal or brass, $350-700.

NORRIS PLANES

Models with the prefix "A" are adjustable. d/t = dovetailed steel

Smooth plane, handled, d/t
most models, $350-750.
gunmetal 50G, $500-1000.

Panel plane, 13½" - 17½", d/t
most models, $500-1200.
An early A1 sold at a 1999 auction for $3405 (FINE).

Jointer plane 20½" - 24½", d/t (similar to the panel plane), $2000-4000.

Note: These planes were made up to 28½", but are very rare over 24½".

Shoulder plane

most models, $225-450.

A7, d/t, $500-900.

gunmetal, $400-650.

Bullnose plane

iron, $150-250.

gunmetal, $250-400.

A27, gunmetal, $1250-1750.

Chariot plane

iron, $200-350.

gunmetal, $350-600.

A28, gunmetal, $1500-2500.

Miter plane

#11, d/t, $2000-3500.

MATHIESON and SPIERS PLANES

Similar to the non-adjustable Norris models
d/t = dovetailed steel

Smooth plane, handled, d/t, $200-450.

Panel plane, 13½"-17½", d/t, $300-700.

Jointer plane, 20½" - 24½", d/t, $750-1500.

Shoulder plane, d/t, $175-325.

Miter plane, d/t, $500-1000.

Improved pattern miter plane, d/t, *right*, $350-700.

There are subtle differences in any model: an improved pattern miter plane, identical to the one above, except the mouth was skewed, brought $2719 at auction.

PRESTON PLANES

d/t = dovetailed steel

Smooth plane, handled, d/t, $150-300.

Shoulder plane, iron, $175-350.

Bullnose plane, iron, $75-150.

Chariot plane, iron, $75-150.

RECORD PLANES

Smooth plane #04, (similar to Stanley #4), $20-40.

Jointer plane #08, (similar to Stanley #8), $50-100.

Shoulder plane #073, $75-150.

Bullnose plane #076, $35-70.

Circular plane #020, (similar to Stanley #20), $75-125.

Combination plane #405, (similar to Stanley #45), $85-125.

MEASURING TOOLS

Priced from GOOD to GOOD+

High visual appeal and technical complexity characterize measuring tools more than most other tool categories.

Since most measuring tools are calibrated to measure distance, angles, levelness, etc., readability is an important factor in determining condition. To qualify for GOOD condition, a measuring tool must measure correctly and legibly. If the numbers are illegible on a rule, or if a level does not have its leveling bubble, the tool must be considered less than GOOD.

❖   ❖   ❖   ❖   ❖   ❖   ❖   ❖   ❖

RULES

The criteria for rules to be considered *at least* GOOD are:

1. Readability. Somewhat difficult to read (but still understandable) on the outside folds; quite readable inside.

2. Tightness. Some looseness acceptable, i.e., the rule need not stay in a position against gravity.

3. Color. Some yellowing in ivory is acceptable. If there is slight staining in either ivory or boxwood, it should not affect readability.

4. Straightness. Warpage over $^1/16$" at any point in the folded position is not acceptable for GOOD.

5. Original condition. Original finish need not be present. Cracks in ivory should not be beyond the hairline stage. Alignment or "closing pins" can be missing.

Variables that can add to the value of a rule, besides ornateness and the rarity of the material used, are the rareness of the maker and the particular model. For information on this, check the specific books listed in the Bibliography. However, one rarity to look for is a rule marked A. STANLEY rather than the later STANLEY trademarks. These are considerably more valuable. See John Walter's book *Antique & Collectible Stanley Tools* for A. Stanley prices.

All rules listed in this chapter, are priced as made of boxwood, except where otherwise specified.

CARPENTER'S RULE

These are by far the most common of the rules, with some models still being made today. Three or four foot rules are found less often than one or two foot ones and, consequently, are valued higher. A three-fold rule (three sections) is rarer than either a two- or four-fold. Six-fold rules are very rare. Rules with metal binding on their edges are generally more valuable than unbound ones. Large "arch-type" brass plates on the joints are more appealing and consequently more valuable than square-ended plates.

Stanley and other American rules that are graduated in metric are more valuable than similar rules in standard English graduations.

As mentioned before, aesthetics is a big factor. Any measuring tool that has an unattractive appearance will sell for considerably less. This is truer with rules than with most other tool categories.

Stanley was the most prolific of the rulemakers and listed below is a representative cross section of the varieties it produced. Other American makers whose rules are often found are Belcher Bros., E.M. Chapin, H. Chapin, Chapin-Stephens, Lufkin, Standard, E.A. Stearns, Stephens Co., Upson Nut, and Winchester. Rabone and Preston are the English equivalents of Stanley in rules. There was a Stanley - London that had no connection with Stanley, USA.

(For carpenter's caliper rules, see page 84.)

Boxwood

Stanley #7, 2-foot, 4-fold, unbound, $40-100.

Stanley #12, 2-foot, 2-fold,
    unbound, with slide, $75-200.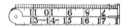

Stanley #15, 2-foot, 2-fold, brassbound, with slide, (similar to #12), $100-225.
Stanley #58, 2-foot, 6-fold, unbound, $250-450.
Stanley #61, 2-foot, 4-fold, unbound, $10-20.

Stanley #62, 2-foot, 4-fold, brassbound, $20-40.

Stanley#65, 1-foot, 4-fold, unbound, $50-150.
Stanley #65½, 1-foot, 4-fold, brassbound, $75-200.

Stanley #66½, 3-foot, 4-fold, unbound, $12-25.

Stanley #66¾, 3-foot, 4-fold, brassbound, $30-60.

Stanley #68, 2-foot, 4-fold, unbound, $8-15.

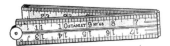

Stanley #84, 2-foot, 4-fold, half-bound brass, i.e., outside edges only are bound, $12-25.

Stanley #94, 4-foot, 4-fold, brassbound, $100-200.

Three-fold with level, $100-200.

Four-fold with level and protractor hinge, $75-150.

Ivory

Stanley #85, 2-foot, 4-fold, unbound, German silver trim, (similar to #87), $250-500.

Stanley #87, 2-foot, 4-fold, German silver bound, $325-600.

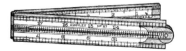

Stanley #88, 1-foot, 4-fold, German silver bound, (similar to #92), $200-400.

Stanley #90 or #92, 1-foot, 4-fold, unbound, German silver trim, $175-350.

Stanley #93, 6", 2-fold, unbound, German silver trim, $250-500.

Non-Stanley Maker
6", 2-fold, unbound, brass trim, $75-200.
1-foot, 4-fold, unbound, brass trim, $100-225.
2-foot, 4-fold, unbound, brass trim, $150-275.

Maple

Zigzag, European, metric, *left,* $20-40.

Zigzag, American, 6-foot, *lower right.*

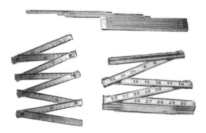

As there are well over 100 Stanley models of zigzag rules, varying in price from $5 to $500, it is best to consult John Walter's book for individual prices. Most run around $25. The metric ones are the most valuable.

Sliding interlock, *upper right,* $15-30.

<u>LUMBER RULE</u>   (generally made of maple or hickory)

Although it is difficult to tell the difference between a board rule, a log rule, and a cruising stick, a description of their characteristics, along with illustrations, can be found in *Collecting Antique Tools.*

To be considered GOOD the numbers must be legible. The iron or brass "hooks" found at the end of some lumber rules are critical to their use and, if missing, reduces the condition to below GOOD. Some lumber rules signed by Hoyt, Chapin-Stephens, or Sanborn will sell for 25-50% over the prices shown below, (and more for rules 5 feet and over). Rules by Haselton have sold as high as $350 for rare models in FINE condition.

Board rule
　　flat stick, 3-4 ft.,　$20-45.
　　with peg holes for tallying, *top,*　$30-60.
　　with round "hooked" end, *center,*　$30-60.
　　octagonal, *bottom,*　$50-100.
　　springy, with "double hook," *A- top,*　$30-60.

Log rule
　　"International Log Rule," *A-center,*　$20-45.
　　square stick, 3-4 ft.,　$35-70.

Cruising stick, most often marked
　　"Cruising Stick," *A-bottom*,　$40-80.

A

PATTERNMAKER'S SHRINK RULE

Stanley #30½A through #30½M
　　each a 24" rule with shrinkage rates ranging from ½" to ⅛" (shown on the rule near the maker's name or model number),　$20-45.

ENGINEER'S RULE

Double slide rule, complex, *center,*　$125-250.

Single slide rule, *top,*　$75-175.

Stanley #53½ architect's rule, *bottom*,　$50-100.

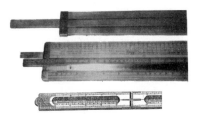

Gunter-type rule
　　without slide, *right,*　$50-100.
　　with slide. See Carpenter's Rules, Stanley #12 and #15.
　　A "top of the line" Gunter-type ivory slide rule with German silver fittings sold for $2600 at auction.

Proof slide rule (for alcohol calculations), similar to single Engineer's rule.

    boxwood, $50-100.

    ivory, $100-225.

    boxwood & ivory, $75-175.

    double slide ivory, $150-300.

NAVIGATIONAL RULE

Sector rule

    ivory, *top*, $60-120.

    boxwood, $35-70.

Map rule

    ivory, *bottom*, $35-70.

    boxwood, $20-40.

Parallel rule

    6" ebony, *top left*, $15-25.

    12"-18" ebony, *center*, $20-45.

    6" ivory and ornate brass, *top center*, $100-200.

    6" ivory with center bar, *top right*, $100-200.

    6" ivory, plain and without center bar, $50-100.

    18"-24" boxwood, *bottom*, $50-100.

Rolling parallel

    12"-18", all brass, *top*, $60-100.

    12"-15", ebony, ivory and brass, *bottom*, $125-200.

    12"-15", boxwood or ebony, $75-150.

CALIPER RULE

Although most of these rules are considered carpenter's rules, all types of caliper rules are included in this section.

Boxwood

    rope rule, 6" x 2½", *top left*, $65-125.

    spoke and axle rule, 6" x 2", *top right*, $65-125

    wire rope rule, 4" x 2¼", *bottom*, $50-100.

    Stanley #32, 1-foot, 4-fold, $20-40.

Stanley #36, 6", 2-fold, (similar to #32), $12-25.

Stanley #36½, 1-foot, 2-fold, $20-40.

Ivory

Stanley #38, 6", 2-fold, unbound,
German silver trim, $150-275.

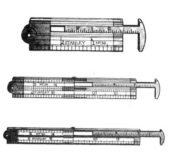

Stanley #39, 1-foot, 4-fold, unbound,
German silver trim, $200-400.

Stanley #40, 1-foot, 4-fold,
German silver bound, $175-350.

Non-Stanley Maker
1-foot, 4-fold, German silver bound, (similar to Stanley #40), $100-250.
1-foot, 4-fold, unbound, (similar to Stanley #39), $85-200.
6", 2-fold, unbound (similar to Stanley #38), $75-150.

WANTAGE RULE & GAUGING ROD

Wantage rule
hinged, *top*, $60-120.
patented Eli S. Primes, *bottom*, $225-400.
solid rod type, $40-80.

Gauging rod, sectional, brass and boxwood,
center, $100-200.

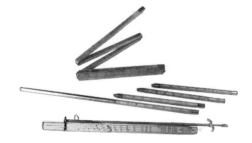

TAILOR'S RULE

Curved, *top*, $35-70.

Solid, *center*, $25-45.

Foldable, *bottom*, $30-60.

COMBINATION RULE

Slight pitting and some rust is allowed on the blade for GOOD condition. Some staining of the boxwood and tarnishing of the brass is also acceptable.

Stephens Co. #36 (similar to Chapin-Stephens #036, next page), $150-250.

Note: A Stephens Co. ivory and German silver inclinometer rule (similar to Stephens #36) sold at auction for $3750, along with an L. C. Stevens brass and ebony one for $4000.

Chapin-Stephens Co. #036, $150-225.

Stanley #036 (similar to Chapin-Stephens #036), $350-550.

Winter and others (English), $300-500.

OTHER RULES

Only a few of the vast variety of specialized rules, are listed below.

Cloth dissector, *top,* $60-100.

Diagram square, *center,* $30-60.

Hat rule, *bottom,* $45-90.

Foot rule
>   *top,* $30-60.
>   *center,* $40-80.
>   18th century sliding extension type, *bottom,* $125-200.

Brass ornate joint rule (depending upon ornateness), $50-125.

Advertising rule, (price is affected by size and advertising content), $5-50.

Blacksmith's rule similar to brass ornate joint rule but without ornate joint, $20-40.

Stanley #1 "Odd Job"

>with correct 12" solid rule, $125-225.
>without rule, $65-125.

PLUMB BOBS

Two criteria affecting the price of plumb bobs are shape and size. Unusual shapes and plumb bobs over 6" in overall length command higher prices. Also important is the material used, e.g., brass vs. iron, the age of the bob, and especially eye appeal.

Most brass bobs have screw-off steel tips and brass tops. For a condition grade of GOOD the tops must be removeable (with effort is okay) but the tips not necessarily so. Minor nicks and tarnish are acceptable. Separate wooden reels (for the string) increase the price $12-25, while bone or brass reels increase the price $25-50.

Listed below are the plumb bobs shown, reading from left to right. All bodies are brass, unless otherwise noted. The price ranges are unusually wide in order to accommodate size differences. The lower end is at approximately 3" in length, unless otherwise stated.

External bobbin or reel type, $85-200.

Turnip-shaped
>up to 6", $50-125.
>over 6", $100-250.

Elongated with ball top, $40-100.

Conical, large, over 6", $30-75.

Ribbed body with turned top, $75-175.

Conical, medium, 3"-6", $12-35.

Reverse conical, $60-150.

Ornately turned and knurled, $125-350.
>*Note: A very fine 6" bob, impressively decorated and dated 1835, sold at a 1994 auction for $1600.*

Teardrop
>iron, $35-75.
>brass, $50-150.

Conical, narrow, $12-35.

Combination cylinder and ball, $35-75.

Conical, without elongated top
>iron, $5-10.
>brass, $15-60.

(three following are continued from previous page)

Carrot-shaped, early, $60-125.

Pear-shaped, 6" and over, $125-325.

Combination conical and ball, $35-75.

Others:

Miniatures (under 3"), $25-60.

Bulbous with long tapered tip
> up to 6", $25-60.
> over 6", $50-175.

Hexagonal, $15-35.

Pointed cylinder, $10-30.

Reversible (top and bottom ends can be unscrewed and reversed), $100-225.

Internal bobbin, $125-300.

Ivory: A caution concerning ivory plumb bobs. Many were made for decorative purposes only and are still being made today from pool balls. However, the ones from the 19th century are sought after by collectors. *A presentation ivory bob, with gold and silver inlaid into tortoise shell, brought $3040 at a 1995 auction.* The more common ivory bobs, even those classified as "contemporary," run between $150 and $300.

LEVELS

Wooden levels prices are heavily influenced by the type of wood and the amount of brass trim used. Woods most often found in levels, in ascending order of value, are: cherry, mahogany, rosewood, and ebony. Brass end and side plates were used in better levels, with full brass edge binding appearing on the highest quality models. Dents and scratches consistent with normal use, and tarnished brass are acceptable for GOOD.

Cast iron levels are often found with breaks in their decorative castings and chips on their edges and corners. A ¼" missing corner will downgrade an otherwise FINE example to GOOD, and two or more broken corners, or missing pieces of decorative filigree, will move it down to GOOD MINUS. Some of these iron levels have inclinometers with tiny dials to indicate the angle of incline. Frozen (jammed) inclinometers are common and will almost always loosen upon disassembly. This condition will normally not degrade the level below GOOD.

The all-important part of the level, wood or iron, is its vials or "bubbles." A level with a broken or missing vial will bring its condition down one grade.

CARPENTER'S WOODEN SPIRIT LEVEL

Stanley, brassbound, rosewood

18"-30", **B**-*top*, $100-200.

Original finish counts high in levels. A 24" with 99% original finish in FINE condition sold for $775 at auction.

12", $125-250.

9", $250-450.

6", $400-650.

Stanley, brassbound, mahogany

24"-30", $50-100.

B

Stanley, unbound, 24"-30"

rosewood, $50-100.

mahogany, $20-50.

cherry, $10-30.

Because of the many models in each of the groups above, it is desireable to check out individual prices in Walter's price guide. The prices above are generalized from the **more common models.**

Stratton Bros., brassbound, rosewood

22"-30", $100-200.

12", $150-225.

10", $175-250.

8", $200-300.

6½", $300-450.

Stratton Bros., brassbound, mahogany, 22"-30" (similar to above), $50-100.

Akron Eclipse, brassbound, mahogany, 12", **B**-*bottom*, $50-100.

L.L. Davis, mahogany, 15", **B**-*center*, $30-60.

Davis & Cook, mahogany, 30", $35-70.

Listed on the following page are a few more of the level manufacturers the collector might come upon. The levels priced are the 24" - 30" length with a center horizontal bubble and one plumb (vertical) bubble. Most of these levels have brass side plates (protecting the center bubble) and brass end or butt plates. The more brass, the more toward the upper end of the price range. None are edge bound, unless stated.

Those found mostly in cherry:

Chapin (various initials), $12-30.

Chapin-Stephens Co. or C.S. Co., $12-30.

Disston & Sons (various name modifications), $20-50.

Keen Kutter, $20-50.

Sargent, $10-25.

Standard Rule, $12-30.

Winchester, $45-90.

Craftsman-made, $8-20.

Those found mostly in mahogany:

Disston & Morss, $30-75.

Goodell-Pratt, brassbound, $40-80.

Hall & Knapp, $60-125.

J.W. Harmon, $50-100.

Mulliken & Stackpole, $40-80.

D.M. Lyon, $40-80.

H.M. Pool, $45-90.

L.B. Watts, $35-70.

Craftsman-made, $15-30.

Note: A signed level of oversize proportions, in mahogany, sold in a private sale (1991) for $3800. It had the most ornate brass inlay ever seen on a level (for that matter on any tool), proving that "looks" is a very important factor in pricing.

English (e.g., Rabone, Preston, Marples) and

Scottish (e.g., Mathieson, Marshall)

brass and mahogany with end vial, *top,* $50-100.

brass and mahogany, *second from top,* $30-60.

brass and rosewood (similar to one above), $40-80.

brass and ebony, *second from bottom,* $45-90.

brass and ebony, *bottom,* $50-100.

brass and ebony ornate, *top,* $60-125.

brass and rosewood, ornate, $50-100.

brass and ebony very ornate, *bottom,* $100-200.

CARPENTER'S CAST IRON SPIRIT LEVEL

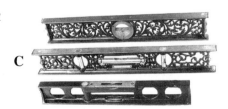

Davis Level & Tool Co.   C

level 18", *C-middle,* $100-200.

level 6" (similar to C-middle), $150-300.

inclinometer, 12" - 24", *prev. pg. **C**- top,* $200-325.

Wider inclinometer models (slightly over 3") and those with decorative gilt, bring above 50% more for each of these characteristics. *A wider model (possibly a presentation piece) with more ornate filigree and decorative gilt and engraving brought $3800 at auction.*

7", (similar to 12"-24" above) $225-350.

6", "mantle-clock" style, *D-bottom,* $225-325.

D

Stanley #36
9" - 24", $15-35.

6", $30-60.

Nicholson patent (Stanley), 14" - 24", *prev. pg. **C**-bottom,* $100-225.
Note: A Nicholson patent level with a rare rotating vial assembly sold at auction for $1100. The slight difference between specific models can mean a great difference in price.

Mellick patent inclinometer, depending on the decorativeness (usually a mahogany base), $350-700.
*A cast iron model (**D**-top) sold at a 1998 auction for $2300, and for $3630 in 2000 (in almost similar conditions).*

POCKET LEVEL

top left, $10-20.
bottom left, $15-35.
top right, $30-60.
center right, $45-100.
bottom right, $12-25.

Some signed ones can be quite valuable. *A Stratton level, similar to the bottom left, sold in a 2000 auction for $1100,*

Davis Level & Tool Co., 2½" - 3½" - 4½"
with iron acorn finials on both ends, $100-200.
with brass finials a 3¾" model sold for $475 in a 2000 auction.

MACHINIST LEVEL

Since very sensitive vials are an integral element of a machinist's level, the tool is downgraded if the bubble has been replaced improperly or tampered with.

top, $150-250.

center, $35-70.

bottom, **Stanley #39½,** or

     Stanley #38½, $20-40.

Davis Level & Tool Co. "pedestal" type

   4" long, $150-250.

Starrett "pedestal" type, 8"-12" long (similar to center above but without top bar) $35-70.

LEVEL and GRADE FINDER

Many of these levels have the needle dial missing or broken, and/or the dial face unreadable. These faults will downgrade the tool to GOOD MINUS. A sticking compass needle is acceptable for GOOD, but broken internal sighting parts are not. Be sure you know the correct angle to look into the top sighting hole before condemning the internal sights. Some staining is OK for GOOD.

Helb's patent, $225-350.

MASON'S LEVEL

36"-48" bound (modern), $12-25.

36"-42" unbound, Stanley #70 or #80, $15-30.

SQUARES

For common squares and bevels, it's appearance that sells the tool: its brass facings and inlays, rich-looking wood (preferably rosewood), and a minimum of oxidation of the blade. Often complexity is the prized variable – the more things the tool can do with its added components, the more valuable it is.

GOOD condition allows tarnished brass, an oxidized but not pitted blade, minor dents and scratches in the wood, and a small check or two.

FRAMING or ROOFING SQUARE

Take-down (must be capable of disassembly), *left*, $40-80.

Handforged, handstruck numbers, usually 18th c., *right,* $20-50.
   dated (early 1800s), $75-150.

One-piece roofing square, similar to one at right except late model, $5-10.

TRYSQUARE

(The more elaborate the brass trim, the more valuable.)

Rosewood, brassbound
   3" blade, *center,* $15-35.
   6" - 12" blade, $10-40.
   15" - 18" blade, with tab or pin in handle, *top,* $40-100.
   20" - 24" blade, with tab or pin in handle, $60-150.
   15" - 18" blade, with level in handle, $75-175.

E

Mahogany, brassbound, 6"- 12" blade, $5-15.

Ebony, brassbound, 6"- 12" blade, $20-50.

Rosewood or mahogany, brass framed (wood is inset into brass frame), $50-125.

Topp's framing square, $90-150.

Machinist, all steel, 4"- 6" blade, *prev. pg,* ***E***-*bottom,* $10-20.

All wood, 6" - 10" blade, $8-25.

12" - 18" blade, $25-50.

MITER SQUARE

Specialty, pierced holes in blade, *top,* $25-50.

Rosewood, brassbound
bottom, $12-30.

blade at 45° angle to handle, $30-70.

T-SQUARE (up to 48")

maple or mahogany (double the price for rosewood or ebony)

fixed head, $8-15.

moveable head, $25-50.

laminated with different colored woods, $25-50.

BEVELS

Bevels have just about the same condition criteria as squares. However, bevels have a moving blade and almost all squares do not. That introduces the screw and nut or wingnut that fixes the blade to the handle. Many times they have been replaced, and if so, the new part is almost always improper. You can usually tell by the new and awkward look to the replaced part. It just doesn't look as if it belongs. This will degrade the tool to GOOD MINUS.

WOOD BEVEL

All wood, $8-20.

SLIDING BEVEL

Rosewood, brassbound (not brass framed)
> single-bladed, L.D. Howard (brass stepped at top)
>> *right,* $20-50.
>
> single-bladed (flat brass trim <u>without</u> step at top), $10-30.
> double-bladed, Witter's patent, *left,* $275-450.

Brass framed with rosewood infill

> St. Johnsbury Tool Co., *at right,* $275-450.
>> all steel body, 100-200.

> L.D. Howard cast brass with level, $200-325.
>> cast brass without level, *at right*, $175-275.
>> framed, with level, $150-250.
>> framed, without level, $125-225.

> I.J. Robinson, $125-225.

SHIPBUILDER'S BEVEL

Brass and boxwood, *at right*, $25-50.

Brass and rosewood, $35-70.

Stanley #42 (similar to boxwood above), $45-90.

COMBINATION SQUARE and BEVEL

Ritchie's patent
> German silver and mahogany, $250-500.
> German silver and rosewood, $350-600.
> German silver and ebony, $450-750.

Complex combination, *top,* $125-200.

W.F. Fisher patent, *bottom left,* $500-800.

F.H. Coe Mfgr., *right,* $150-275.

Langlais patent, $200-325.

CALIPERS, DIVIDERS & COMPASSES

Most of these are metal. To be graded GOOD they must have all their original parts (wing screws, etc.) and must be moveable, even if heavy force is required. Moderate, over-all pitting degrades the tool to GOOD MINUS.

OUTSIDE CALIPER

Machinist style, 6"-12", *right*, $7-15.

Wing style, *left,*

    chamfered or decorated

        15" - 18", $25-50.

        24", $40-80.

    plain

        15" - 18", $15-30.

        6" - 10", $8-15.

Friction style

    handforged, 7", *center,* $15-30.

    locking scale, decorative cut-outs, 8" - 12" over-all, *top,* $25-50.

    locking bar, 11" over-all, *bottom,* $20-40.

    wheelwright or patternmaker's, 30", $40-80.

INSIDE CALIPER

Spring style, 4" - 8", $6-12.

DOUBLE CALIPER

Handforged
  with locking circle and thumb screws, *right,* $85-175.
  without locking circle, friction set, $40-80.

Sheet metal formed, friction set, $20-40.

DANCING MASTER CALIPER   (also called ladylegs or legs caliper)

The more whimsical and "arty," the higher the value. Brass generally brings more than steel, unless the steel caliper shows more age.

Clockwise from top:
  large, handforged, bowlegged, $50-125.
  chubbylegs, $50-125.
  lady-like, $60-150.
  simple, *center,* $30-70.
  balletstyle, $60-150.
  combination, $40-80.
  full silhouette, $150-350,
      depending upon form and age.

LOG CALIPER

Some checks and stains are acceptable for GOOD. The scale must be mostly readable. Brass can be tarnished.

Factory-made, *left,* $75-150.

Craftsman-made, plain, *right,* $25-50.

Craftsman-made, fine, $50-125.

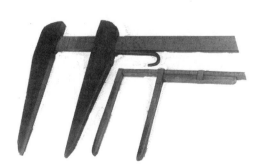

Fabian mfgr., $75-150.

Hoyt mfgr., (usually all cherry), $65-125.
 A full paper label of instructions on the arm has
 brought as much as a 100% premium.

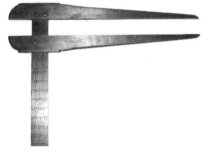

Greenleaf mfgr.
 with pinwheel, $1500-2250.
 without pinwheel, $300-600.

Haselton mfgr., iron jaws,
 brass slide, $125-225.

WOODEN DIVIDER

Wing style
 10", *left,* $30-60.
 18", $50-100.
 30", $100-200.

Cooper's, bent, French style, *top right,* $150-300.

METAL DIVIDER

Cooper's, handforged, $30-60.

Wing style

handforged, plain, *top,* $25-50.
handforged, decorative, *bottom,* $45-90.
late factory model, $6-15.

Dated tools always bring a premium. Some dividers dated in the 1700s brought $400 - 800, depending upon how early the date was.

figure eight, brass, *top,* $175-300.
decorative rosewood and brass, *bottom,* $100-200.

Stoddard patent, brass body, steel legs, $50-100.

Friction style, handforged, early
    plain, *right,* $12-25.
    decorative, $50-100.

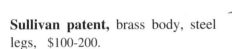

Sullivan patent, brass body, steel legs, $100-200.

French "compasses," iron
    plain legs, 15"-24", *left,* $150-300.
    fancy legs, 15"-20", *center,* $250-500.
    fancy legs, 22"-30", *right,* $400-800.

PROPORTIONAL DIVIDER

Brass, $30-50.

German silver, $40-70.

BEAM COMPASS or TRAMMELS

Wooden trammel points need the beam to give them the right look, while the ornate metal points (usually brass) seem to sell almost as well on their own, without the beam. Most beams are wood, with a few made of brass or steel. The more unusual and attractive the design, and the larger the size, the higher the price in the range shown. However, if the "keepers" are missing (the U-shaped pressure protectors between the screw and the beam), the piece loses a grade.

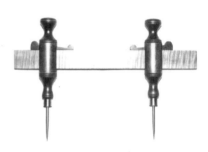

Wood body, steel tips, 4"-12" over-all,
    depending on the type and workmanship, $35-75.

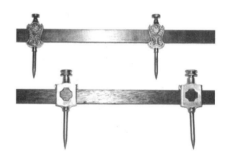

Brass body, steel tips,
    cast floral design, *top*, $45-90.

    pierced design, *bottom*, $40-100.

    plain rectangle, $25-65.

    large (7" or more over-all), geometric or fancy
      design, $100-300.
        depending on size and ornateness.

GAUGES and SLITTERS

GOOD condition requires that all the marking spurs or cutters be present (although not necessarily sharpened) and that the mortising spur adjusting screw (that moves one of the spurs) actually works. An improper thumbscrew downgrades the tool to GOOD MINUS.

Two major criteria of value are the amount of brass and the type of wood. The preferred woods are, in ascending order: beech, maple, apple, mahogany, boxwood, rosewood, and ebony.

MARKING GAUGE

Brass wear plate in fence
beech or maple, *right,* $8-20.
mahogany, $10-25.
rosewood or boxwood, $20-40.

Without brass wear plate
beech or maple, *right,* $5-10.
mahogany, $7-15.
rosewood or boxwood, $12-25.

MORTISE GAUGE

Brass wear plates in fence
mahogany, $15-45.
boxwood, $25-60.
rosewood, $30-70.
ebony, *top left,* $35-80.

Marsden patent, *top right,* $150-300.

Full brass fence, *bottom,* $40-100.

Blaisdell patent, *top left,* $175-325.

Williams patent, *top right,* $150-300.

Sholl patent, *bottom,* $175-325.

Round brass stem, oval ebony fence with full brass plate,
$50-80.

Stanley #92, *top,* $50-100.

Stanley #98, *bottom,* $10-25.

"Grasshopper" or wheelwright style, *left,* $15-35.

Continental style, *right,* $15-35.

PANEL GAUGE

Tiger maple, ivory wear plate, *left,* $50-100.

Rosewood and brass, *right,* $50-100.

Without brass trim
> beech or maple, $10-20.
> mahogany, $15-35.
> rosewood, $25-60.

With brass trim, 50% added to any of the above.
With handle, 50% added to any of the above.

FLOORING GAUGE   (previously called Clapboard Gauge)

These gauges look like panel gauges with many steps cut into the fence. They were used mostly for flooring work, even though they have been called clapboard gauges for many years. Most are craftsman-made. *A double-sided one, signed by J.F. Bauder (a rare planemaker) sold at a 1991 auction for $1200.*

> steps cut on a flat side, *right,* $35-75.
> steps cut on a concave side, $50-100.

CLAPBOARD GAUGE

Nesters patent, brass faced mahogany, with level,
> $250-400.

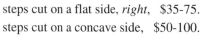

Stanley #88, $12-30.

Stanley #89, $20-50.

SLITTER

Some liberties were taken when slitters were included among measuring tools. They were included because their look and manner of use are close enough to be considered "family."

Wedged blade
> no brass trim or wear plate, *top,* $10-20.
> brass wear plate and trim
>> mahogany, $15-30.
>> boxwood or rosewood, $30-60.
>> ebony, *bottom,* $40-80.

Handled

no brass trim, $20-40.

brass trim, $30-60.

Rice's patent, $250-375.

Leatherworker's draw gauge

rosewood and brass, $45-85.

all iron, $20-35.

Note: An Osborne draw gauge, requiring a special casting for left-handed use, sold for $1050 in a 1997 auction.

Leatherworker's plow, $75-150.

TRAVELERS

Travelers are among the few tools that go against the rule that a manufactured signed piece is more valuable than a homemade one. Handforged travelers bring more than factory-cast ones. Ornate patterns or brass wheels command the highest prices. They are often treated as folk art and decorative wall hangings.

TRAVELER, CRAFTSMAN-MADE

Starwheel, *left,* $75-125.

Heart and star wheel, *top,* $100-225.

Center bar wheel, *bottom,* $35-60.

Brass wheel, $85-175.

Solid metal wheel, $25-50.

Solid wooden wheel, $30-60.

TRAVELER, FACTORY-MADE

Cast wheel, with pointer, $30-50.

SAWS

Priced from GOOD to GOOD+

Several factors besides condition affect the price of saws. The smaller types such as jewelers' saws and fret saws are also judged on their aesthetic qualities. Mid-sized saws, such as carpenters' handsaws, while valued for their appearance (particularly the detailing and the wood used in their handles), are also affected by their functional ability, since they are often bought for use. The larger saws, such as pit saws, though attractive and rare, don't enjoy the prices and popularity you might expect, because of their space requirements.

A saw in GOOD condition can be covered with light oxidation, dull, a tooth or two chipped, frame warped or handles checked, but it must be complete.

TWO-MAN SAWS

CROSS-CUT TIMBER SAW

5' - 6', $20-40.

3' - 4', $15-30.

PIT SAW and PLANK SAW

Framed plank saw, 6' over all by approx. 1½' wide. $150-300.

Pit saw
> framed, 8' over all by approx. 2½' wide, $400-800.
> open, *right,* approx. 7' blade
> > with both upper and lower handles, $150-300.
> with upper handle, but without lower handle, $85-200.

VENEER SAW

Framed veneer saw, smaller and lighter than the plank saw, with a parallel width blade as opposed to the tapered blade of the plank or pit saw, $85-200.

ONE-MAN TWO-HANDED SAWS

ICE SAW

4' - 5' blade, $40-80.
  (shown with handle disassembled)

BUCK SAW

36"- 42" blade, $20-40.
24"- 30" blade, $15-30.

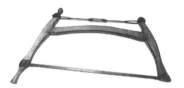

BOW SAW

Replaced toggle sticks are OK for GOOD. Boxwood handles, elaborate toggle sticks, heavy chamfers, and small sizes (blades 12" or under), move the value to the high end of the range.

beech, maple, $35-70.

fruitwood, mahogany, $60-120.

rosewood, $75-200
  A whalebone bow saw sold at a 1999 auction for $2600.

FRAMED SAW (Turning or Felloe Saw)

Warpage is OK for GOOD

With ram's horn nuts, $40-80.
With standard square head nuts, $25-50.

STAIR SAW

classic shape

    beech, *top,* $25-65.

    mahogany or fruitwood, *bottom,* $40-85.

fancy shape, $60-150.

fancy carvings, $75-200.

    Note: A craftsman-made stair saw with a bird carved on the front was sold at a non-tool auction as folk art for $1100.

ONE-HANDED SAWS

HANDSAW

Cross-cut and Rip

    early and signed, *bottom,* $35-150.

        depending on the rarity of the maker, degree of engraving, and look of the handle.

    later, *top,* $5-20.

        based on useability.

    saw with level and scriber in the handle, $275-450.

    Note: A Disston #43 combination saw, with vertical and horizontal levels, sold for $1350 in a 1997 auction.

    saw with rosewood handle, $75-150.

BACK SAW   (higher prices based greatly on signature)

Miter, closed handle

    steel back, $25-85.

    brass back, $35-125.

Tenon, open handle

    steel back, $20-75.

    brass back, $30-100.

Dovetail, straight handle

    steel back, $15-50.

    brass back, $25-75.

Miter box (without Backsaw), $25-75,
based on complexity.

Back saws by Philadelphia makers such as W. Toland, Johnson & Conaway,
W. & C. Johnson, Dilworth Branson & Co., and Wm. McNiece: $65-175.

FRET or COPING SAW

Sorrento patent, *left*, $100-175.

Woodframe, *right*
beech or maple, $25-60.
rosewood, $100-200.

Metal frame

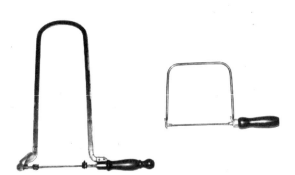

deep throat, toggle, *left*, $20-45.

modern style, *right*, $4-10.

COMPASS SAW

Early, $25-50.

Later, $7 -15.

PAD or KEYHOLE SAW

beech, maple, $12-25.

rosewood, boxwood, $20-40.

ebony, $25-50.

PATTERNMAKER'S SAW

$35-70.

JEWELER'S SAW

small, 9" over all,   *top,* $12-25.

large, 15" over all,   *bottom,* $15-30.

HACKSAW

Lancashire pattern, *top,* $25-50.

Craftsman, well made, *middle,* $20-40.

Early English, signed, *bottom,* $25-50.

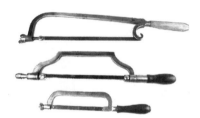

Modern, $5-10.

FLOORING SAW

$40-75.

SAWSETS

There are over 800 sawset patents. For further information see *Patented American Sawsets* (in Bibliography).

Chase patent, pliers style, *top left,* $75-150.

Comb or wrest style, *bottom left,* $10-20.

Stillman patent, pliers style, *top right,* $6-12.

Morrill's patent, pliers style, *bottom right,* $7-15.

Large complex, patent, hammer style, $50-120.

Stanley #42, $5-12

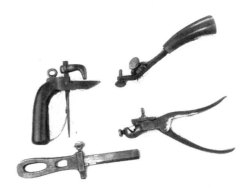

OTHER TOOLS

Priced from GOOD to GOOD+

As there are varieties of tool types in this chapter, specific condition explanations will be discussed before each type.

TAPS and SCREWBOXES

Taps and screwboxes are collected mostly for their historical importance in the development of woodworking rather than for use. Although some factory-made screwboxes were made of boxwood or rosewood, these are by far the exceptions. Most were beech or maple.

GOOD condition in a tap could include a tap that will not cut cleanly. Very few of the early taps have survived in working condition. Most screwboxes can have their blades sharpened and be put into working condition. To be considered GOOD a screwbox must have all its parts available so as to be made functional.

As early taps and screwboxes were made as sets, without consideration of standard thread size or pitch, they are not interchangeable. Although one without the other is functionally worthless, they do have collectible value as separate pieces. For matched sets, add 25% to each of the two parts.

TAP

Standard type
up to 1½" thread diameter, $10-20.

over 1½" thread diameter, $20-40.

End grain type, $15-45.

SCREWBOX

up to 1½" thread diameter, $30-60.
over 1½" thread diameter, $60-120.

111

HAMMERS and MALLETS

To be classified as GOOD hammers and mallets do not need their original handles, but the replacements must have the proper shape. Needless to say, original handles, particularly on the patented models, (or if the handle was stamped or labeled) are more valuable. Light rust is acceptable, as are small cracks or splits in the wood and a loose head.

CLAW HAMMER

Framing, *top,* $10-20.

Roman-style, *bottom,* $15-35.

Standard modern style, $3-6.

Cheney patent, nail-holding type, $20-50.

STRAPPED EYE HAMMER

Early, handforged, *right,* $15-35.

Later, factory-made, straighter claws, $12-30.

BALL PEEN HAMMER

Standard machinist, *top,* $4-8.

"Perfect" handle, *bottom,* $25-50.

TINSMITH'S HAMMER

Graceful shape, finely made, $18-35.

Common style, $6-12.

UPHOLSTERER'S HAMMER

"V" slot in rear tip, $15-35.

BLACKSMITH'S HAMMER

Top fuller, *left,* $7-15.

Top swage, *center,* $7-15.

Punch, *right,* $5-10.

COBBLER'S HAMMER

German pattern, *top,* $10-25.

French pattern, *bottom,* $15-30.

Standard pattern, $6-12.

COOPER'S HAMMER

$15-30.

DOUBLE CLAW HAMMER

Unpatented, $60-120.

Patented, forging demarcation lines between the two
sets of claws can generally be seen,
"PAT'D Nov 4,1902" on head, $100-200.

Modern, acetylene welded heads, polished or painted (reproductions), $25-50.
(similar to factory-forged above)

CRATING HAMMER

This is a combination tool, of which there are many varieties.
$15-30.

Note: Those tools with a product name such as Ivory Soap, Post Toasties, Ideal Dog Food, etc., are worth more, $40-90.

SLATER'S TOOLS

Hammer, *top,* $25-50.

Ripper, *bottom,* $20-40.

BRICKLAYER'S HAMMER

$7-15.

MILLPICK   (used for dressing millstones)

$10-20.

MARKING HAMMER

up to 5 lbs., $25-50.

5 lbs and over, $35-75.

FARRIER'S HAMMER

top, $10-20.

SADDLEMAKER'S HAMMER

bottom, $25-60.

SAWYER'S HAMMER

Standard inverted tapered head, *top,* $40-80.

Dual-headed, striking edges at right angles to each other, *center*, $20-40.

Dual-headed, symmetrical, slitted handle, *bottom,* $30-50.

Note: Those with saw company names such as Atkins, Simmonds, Disston, etc., are worth about 50% more.

VENEER HAMMER

Cast iron head, *left,* $30-60.

Forged head, *right,* $40-80.

Wooden head, $25-50.

Brass head, $40-80.

CARPENTER'S MALLET

Cylinder, *left,* $15-45, based on type of wood.
   Lignum, rosewood, and burls are highest in value.

Tapered rectangle, $10-35, based on size.

CARVER'S MALLET

Turned spherical, lignum, *right,* $30-60.

Tapered cylinder, $20-50, based on type of wood

CAULKING MALLET and IRONS

Mallet
   oak or hickory, *bottom,* $25-50.
   lignum, $40-80.

Irons
   twisted handle, *second from bottom,* $15-30.
   flared, *second from top,* $5-10.
   hawsing, *top,* $20-40.

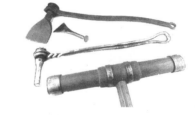

WHEELWRIGHT'S MALLET

   $10-20.

BILL POSTING HAMMER

Robertson patent, 1886, $90-250.
   one to four section handle; highest value in four sections.

FILEMAKER'S HAMMER

   $75-165.

SILVERSMITH'S and COPPERSMITH'S HAMMER

Repousse hammer, *top,* $25-50.

JEWELER'S HAMMER

Flat poll, fancy handle, *center,* $30-60.

WATCHMAKER'S HAMMER

bottom, $15-35.

BUNG STARTER

Cooper's mallet, $25-50.

DECORATIVE HAMMER

Hennig patent, 1901, $90-175.

Goat's Head, cast brass, $100-200.
(The proper handle is a simple dowel with a round knob at the end, usually painted).

Fish Head, $900-1200

Note: An elaborately forged and turned socketed hammer, dated 1769, brought $4575 in a 1997 English auction.

CLAMPS and VISES

Since these are basically holding devices, their primary value is in their capability to grasp the workpiece firmly. However, where price is concerned, the look of handforged chamfered iron (in the more decorative vises) takes precedence over function.

In the wooden clamps, freedom of movement is the key. GOOD condition can tolerate some chipped threads and a slightly sticky movement, but it cannot accept bound parts that render the tool inoperative.

In the metal vises, the most common problem is the missing outer jaw spring. This is the spring that forces the jaws apart when the vise is being opened. If it is not there, the outer jaw has to be opened manually. This would downgrade its condition to GOOD MINUS.

PARALLEL CLAMP

6"-9" jaws, $8-15.

10"-14" jaws, $12-20.

15"-18" jaws, $15-35.

Note: Parallel clamps with metal threaded rods are of a later vintage. They are worth more to users but less to collectors and decorators.

FURNITURE CLAMP

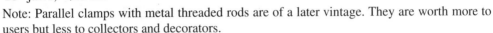

Bar type, *right*

    3' - 4', $12-30.

    5' - 6', $15-35.

Pipe type

    3' - 4', $10-20.

    5' - 6', $12-25.

C-CLAMP (metal)

Standard style, *top*, $6-12.

Speedlock style, *middle*, $10-20.

Miniature, *bottom*, $1-2.

    If the swivel (at the end of the bench clamping threaded rod) is missing, the clamp is no better than GOOD MINUS.

WOODWORKER'S VISE

Early, all wood, *left,* $30-60.

Later, with metal threaded rods and cast iron body, *above right,* $35-70.

Patternmaker's Emmert's patent, $200-350.

MITER JACK

A clamp used for planing at a 45° angle, $60-120.
   The mahogany jack shown is at the top of the range.

METALWORKER'S VISE

Early

blacksmith-made, decorative. Based upon decorativeness and craftsmanship, these vises run between $75-150.
   The one shown is in the upper portion of the range.

blacksmith-made, without fancy forging, $25-50.

Later, factory-made
   5"- 6" high, *bottom,* $10-20.
   6" - 8" high, *right,* $15-30.
   8"- 10" high, *left,* $25-50.

Note: As these vises are more collectible than C-clamps, the missing swivel (at the end of the bench clamping threaded rod) is not as important as on the C-clamp. As such, the lowest price for the range could be tolerated.

BLACKSMITH'S or LEG VISE

These are valued for their craftsmanship in the forging, considering chamfers, etc. If the long curved spring (shown in the center of the vise) is missing, downgrading to the bottom of the range is appropriate.
   $30-60.

HAND VISE

As can be seen in the illustration, there are a goodly number of varieties of this vise, all designed to be held with one hand while working on the piece with the other. Handled models are more valuable.
   $10-40.

SAW VISE   (for sharpening)

All wood, craftsman-made, $10-25.

Manufactured metal style
  toggle type, *right,* $15-30.
  screw type, $10-20.

SCREWDRIVERS

Early turnscrews are valued mostly for their decorative looks. The more the blacksmith sculpted the blade, the better; and the larger it is, the more valuable. Most of these turnscrews have brass ferrules. The tool is downgraded to GOOD MINUS if the ferrule is missing.

The later spiral screwdrivers are utilitarian and are bought mostly by users, who want function, not necessarily looks.

TURNSCREW

Narrow, sculpted, *bottom,* $12-25.

Wide
  sculpted, *second from bottom,* $20-40.
  sculpted, *third from bottom,* $25-50.
  slightly sculpted, *fourth from bottom,* $12-25.
  not sculpted, $7-15.

Miniature, slightly sculpted, *top,* $6-12.

SCREWDRIVER

"Perfect" handle
  with "wings", *left,* $8-15.
  without "wings", $5-10.

Spiral, "Yankee" patent, *middle,* $8-20.

Patent model, lever rod, *right,* $25-45.

Archimedean style (see Archimedean Drills, pg. 7)

TOOL HANDLES

Although these hollow handles with chucks (approximately 6"-7" long) contain screwdriver blades, they may also have chisel blades, saw blades, etc. Usually there are 6-12 blades in total. No blades downgrades to GOOD MINUS.

beech, maple, $12-25.

rosewood, $25-50.

> Some Stanley models are worth up to $100.
>
> (see John Walter's *Antique & Collectible Stanley Tools*, Bibliography.)
>
> *Tool handles from Philadelphia makers, such as John Booth and Bagshaw & Field, complete with all tools and in their original boxes, have sold at auction between $300 and $500.*

WRENCHES

Wrenches have become an increasingly important collectible, boasting a national society and several specialized Guides (see the Bibliography). Many wrenches are patented and have maker name, date, and place of manufacture. It's true that most examples are not much older than 100 years, but that's more than made up for by the great variety of styles, types and sizes and the many intriguing mechanisms.

To be considered GOOD the wrench must function, i.e., it must move (if it has moveable parts) and it must hold in any of its positions. Nicks, cracks in the wooden handle, and rust are all within the GOOD grade. Over-all pitting downgrades to GOOD MINUS. Usually larger sizes are priced at the higher end of the range.

OPEN END and BOX COMBINATION WRENCH

Farm implement, *top,* $20-40.

> *An extremely rare implement wrench, Planet Jr. #312, sold for $1800 at a 2000 Nebraska auction.*

Buggy, *bottom,* $8-15.

MONKEY WRENCH

Coes Wrench Co., one of the more prolific wrench manufacturers, at one time manufactured over one million wrenches a year.

> *bottom,* $8-20.
>
> smallest size, $4^5/8"$, $85-150.

PIPE and MONKEY COMBINATION WRENCH

Bemis & Call Hardware & Tool Co., another important wrench manufacturer.

> *top* (above), $15-30.

PIPE WRENCH

Quick adjusting, *top,* $35-70.

Standard screw type, *middle,* $6-15.

Self adjusting, *bottom,* $12-25.

ALLIGATOR WRENCH

Screw adjusting, *all,* $10-25.

Solid, non-moveable jaws, $4-12.

TWISTED HANDLE NUT WRENCHES

all, $20-50.

SOME UNUSUAL WRENCHES

Combination and angle wrench, *top center,* $250-400.

Ratchet-positioned brace style buggy wrench, *middle,* $100-200.

Lowentraut patent wrench, similar to above, $65-125. (see page 17)

Vertical jaws buggy wrench, *left bottom,* $20-40.

Millea's emergency tool, *right bottom,* $50-100.

COMBINATION TOOL WRENCH

Double pliers and wrench, *left,* $30-60.

Pliers and nut adjusting wrench, *middle,* $35-70.

Pliers and wrench, with filigree casting, *right,* $30-60.

BILLINGS & SPENCER CO. WRENCH

Center-nut adjustment models

10", *A-top,* $12-25.

6", *A-second from left,* $7-15.

8", cutout jaw, *A-far right,* $20-50.

QUICK ADJUSTMENT WRENCH

Steel handle, trigger adjustment, *A-(previous page)*
second from top, $30-60.

Handle adjustment, *A-third from top,* $30-60.

Slide adjustment, *A-fourth from top,* $20-40.

Wood handle, trigger adjustment, *B-third from top,* $85-175.

B

Cam adjustment, *C-top left,* $30-60.

MINIATURE WRENCH

3" long, *A-bottom,* $25-50.

DOUBLE HEADED WRENCH

"S" style, Baxter patent, *B-second from top,* $30-60.

Horizontal jaws, *B-right,* $30-60.

ANGLE WRENCH

Nut adjustment, *C-middle,* $20-40.

Ratchet adjustment, *C-bottom,* $30-60.

C

PLIERS WRENCH

Eifel Plierench, *B-top,* $15-30.

C-jaw, *C-top right,* $15-30.

OPEN HANDLE WRENCH

Decorative body, *B-bottom,* $20-40.

TOOL CHESTS

This is a category with a wide range of prices. A small, plain, non-dovetailed chest with a single tray might sell for about $50, while a top of the line chest will sell for over $5000. A chest similar to the one shown at the end of this section was sold privately for $7500 in 1992.

Collectors use their chests to store the smaller tools in their collections, so size and number of drawers, trays, etc., count. Although apartment dwellers might opt for the smaller size, the larger boxes generally bring more money. The very finest chests are often treated as a piece of furniture, occupying a prominent position in home or office.

Dovetailing, paneling, inlays, marquetry, exotic woods, and crotch or burl veneers all add value. A secret compartment adds not only intrigue but dollars. Finishing items, such as external brass trim, lock and key in working order, ivory or brass draw pulls, etc., all increase the price.

To be considered GOOD a tool chest must be structurally sound, with no rot, no missing drawers or trays, no missing or raised veneer beyond small isolated spots, no split-out of the body at hinged areas. It can have loose hinges, a lock with no key, sticky drawers, a few pieces of missing marquetry, dirty exterior with some paint spatters, missing handles, separated seams in bottom boards, an isolated dovetail breakout, or an isolated nail or screw missing.

A chest that functions well and looks "crisp" would be rated GOOD PLUS and one that has an aesthetically pleasing finish both inside and out, in addition to good functionality and crispness would rate FINE.

To help the reader span the gap from the $50 chest to the $7500 one, the details of various chests are provided.

TOOL CHEST,　　(as shown on page 125)

Size: 36" wide, 27" deep, 26" high.

Outer construction: Dovetailed wide pine with lower mitered base board and upper wide molding strip.

Hardware and trim: Four patent dated cast filigree handles. Lock and key working. Heavy sculpted brass trim around entire lid. Iron 1" "shield points" (9) on outer lid panel.

Inner lid: Raised panels (4) with crotch mahogany. Perimeter: ribbon mahogany and satinwood banding. Inlay and marquetry: ebony, boxwood, mahogany, maple.

Interior sides: Mahogany veneer.

Compartments: Three (one secret).

Compartment dividers: Solid mahogany.

Tills: Four, with brass rollers. (These are the moveable sections that house the drawers).

Drawers: Fifteen, with victorian brass pulls and ebony and boxwood inlays. Crotch mahogany veneer. All dovetailed with beveled bottoms. Twelve additional dummy drawers.

Circa: 1870.

Provenance: Maine.

Condition: FINE.

OTHER TOOL CHESTS

Most chests run from 36" to 42" wide, and 18" to 26" deep or high. There are smaller boxes, but they usually do not have the elaborateness of the sizes listed above. The larger sizes do not necessarily command greater prices unless they are matched with higher quality components, and more elaborate decorativeness. Dovetailed construction of the box and/or its drawers, trays or tills is shown as d/t.

Plain, unveneered interior

non d/t, one tray,	$50-100
non d/t, 2-3 trays,	65-125
d/t, one tray,	75-150
d/t, 2-3 trays,	85-175
d/t, over 3 trays or drawers	100-200

Plain, veneered interior

non d/t, 2-3 trays,	$100-200
d/t, 2-3 trays,	150-300
d/t, 2-6 drawers,	200-400
d/t, 7-12 drawers,	300-600

Veneered with crossbanding or paneled interior, d/t, 6-12 drawers, or 2 or more lidded trays or tills.

no inlays or marquetry,	$400- 800
border inlays,	500-1000
minimum marquetry,	750-1500
elaborate marquetry, or paneling,	1000-2000

Elaborately veneered, crossbanded, d/t, dramatic marquetry, paneled lid, fancy pulls and handles.

6-12 drawers, or two or more tills,	$1500-3000
over 12 drawers,	2000-4000

Chest shown below and described in detail on pages 123-124.

Priced in GOOD to GOOD PLUS condition, (as are those on previous page), $3000-6000.

Priced in actual FINE condition, $7500.

TOOL WOODS

One cold morning at Shupp's Grove, many years ago, I came across a grimy plow plane. "How much?" I asked. The owner said he was looking for $40, "but with all that black paint on it" he would take $30. Turns out that there was no black paint at all. The plow was ebony! I've had similar windfalls with tools of boxwood, rosewood, apple, and other premium woods. It pays to know your woods, not only for value, but for the satisfaction of being able to *completely* identify a tool.

There are many wood identification books on the market, but few supply what the tool collector needs. Hoadley's *Identifying Wood* (Taunton Press) is one of the best, but requires time and effort to learn the wood technologist's language. We don't need to identify all the world's woods, just the twenty or so that were used professionally in tool making. This chapter tries to get through these woods with minimum buzzwords.

The two items that make up **grain**, (as seen by the naked eye), are the longitudinal pores, which form the annual rings, and the rays. The sketch below identifies the rings and rays as they appear in the various sections of the log.

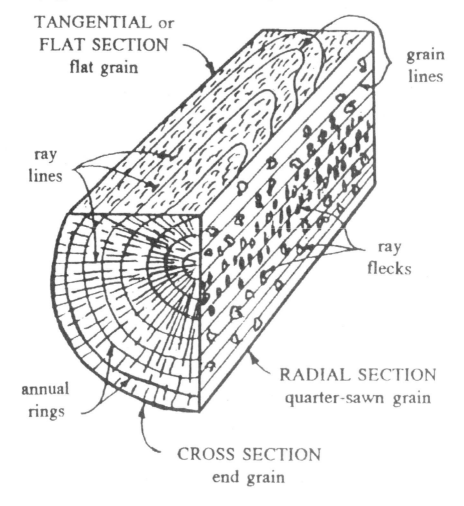

TANGENTIAL or FLAT SECTION
flat grain

grain lines

ray lines

ray flecks

annual rings

RADIAL SECTION
quarter-sawn grain

CROSS SECTION
end grain

Pores are the openings in the tiny tubes running up the tree, that show up as holes when the tree is sawn across the trunk, (cross section). The tree's **annual rings** result from having more, or larger, pores at the start of the growing season. If the pores are readily visible with the naked eye, the wood is termed **open grain**. If 5X magnification is needed, the wood is called **tight** or **close grain.**

The pores appear differently when the log is sawn lengthwise. They are now tiny grooves, such as you would get by cutting a bunch of straws lengthwise. In antique tools these may be filled with grime, making them appear darker. If the cut is through the center of the tree (radial section), the annual rings appear as parallel lines. If the cut is at right angles to the radial section (flat or tangential section), the rings "wander," as in a contour map (see sketch on previous page).

The rays appear solid and flattened and run outward from the center of the tree. In the cross section, they are seen as thin lines running from the core to the bark. In the radial section, they become irregular flecks; in the flat section they are tiny straight lines. The rays are an important identification and usually need 5X magnification.

Two last definitions: the **sapwood** is a doughnut section of wood next to the bark; it is usually much lighter in color than the remaining **heartwood.**

I believe that with just these terms you can identify the 20 or so common tool woods. I've found others: elm, sycamore, honey locust, teak, wenge, cormier, lauan, satinwood, padauk, moradillo, etc., but they are insignificant in tool usage.

The clearest view of the pores and rays requires slicing the wood with a sharp razor. Not likely any of us would ever do this to a tool, unless it could be done on a hidden part. Cleaning the surface with #0000 steelwool will have to suffice. This will also help in determining the true color, as most tools have an aged surface (patina) that deepens their natural color.

Here are the woods:

BOXWOOD, European and Turkish

(current substitutes are: Caribbean and Indonesian)

Almost every tool collector is familiar with the hard homogeneous grain of boxwood rules. Molding plane wear strips, plow planes, and miniatures also use boxwood. When this light yellow to buff wood patinates and darkens, it might be mistaken for maple. Maple's end grain under 5X has very distinct ray lines, while boxwood's rays are so thin and close together that they could be missed even under magnification.

Apple, particularly its sapwood, is occasionally taken for boxwood, but it is much grainier and has a pinkish-brown hue, (as opposed to the yellowish cast of boxwood).

MAPLE, Sugar (also called Rock Maple or Hard Maple)

A sandy-colored wood with tight grain. Rays in the flat section are thin lines about $1/64$ " long. They show as flecks in the radial section. Maple can be found in primitive braces, chisel and other handles, log rules, howels, and crozes. The figured birdseye and tiger grains are seen sometimes in measuring tools. Signed planes in maple are rare.

BEECH, American

This is the most commonly used tool wood, particularly in planes. It is tan in color, but can patinate to a deep walnut. The key to beech is its rays: prominent flecks in the radial section, and thin lines in the flat section (which can go over $1/16$ " long). The fact that the flat-section rays are easily visible to the naked eye helps differentiate beech from birch and maple.

BIRCH, Yellow

Used mostly in early New England planes, it is sometimes confused with beech and maple. It is grainier than either, the flat section showing open pores up to ½" long, (usually darkened with grime). Magnification is needed to see the rays in any section. At 5X they show in the cross section as narrower than the pores. (The rays in maple are the same size as the pores, and in beech they are considerably wider than the pores).

APPLE

Used in planes, an occasional primitive brace, and non-impact handles, particularly saw handles. It has very tight grain, and shows no rays to the naked eye. Its heartwood is pinkish brown; its sapwood much lighter.

CHERRY, Black

Primarily used in levels and non-impact handles, it is grainier than apple. Radial sections show pronounced ray flecks, but none are seen in apple. Cherry's sapwood is light tan, and a stripe of it is generally seen in levels.

HORNBEAM, European

A wood of yellowish-tan cast, common in central European tools, particularly German and Austrian planes and braces. It has wide rays in the radial section, about the width of those in oak. They show as flecks sometimes ¼" wide by an inch long. You'll have to look closely, as the color of the rays is almost the same as the base wood.

HICKORY, various

Used almost exclusively in impact handles, (axes, hammers, etc.). Hickory planes and braces are rare exceptions. Pores are large in diameter and very long in the lengthwise sections, (up to 3"). No rays are visible to the naked eye, which differentiates it from oak. The sapwood is buff and the heartwood light to medium brown.

ASH, various

Not many tools use ash: a plane or two, Dutch and English braces, and some handles. Ash has large pores like hickory and oak, but no rays are visible to the eye, (unlike oak). The heartwood is very light tan. The subtle difference between ash and hickory (besides color), is in the longitudinal pores. In ash they are generally under ½" long, while in hickory they are over ½". Another difference can be seen in the end grain. Ash has a tight cluster of large pores (2 or 3 deep), right at the ring line, while hickory has the pores more distributed between ring lines.

OAK, Red and White

The common red and white oaks are rarely used in any but homemade tools. They have large pores, long rays in the flat section (up to 1" long), and almost a garish ray fleck pattern when quartersawn in the radial section.

OAK, Live

Live oak is much heavier and darker brown than the common oaks, and has a more twisted grain. Its pores are smaller, but its rays in the flat section are thicker and more pronounced. It was used mostly for bench planes. It is on the borderline of sinking; most of the time it will sink slowly.

OAK, Cork

Growing mostly in Spain and Portugal, this tree's bark is harvested for cork. Many of the long shouldered rabbet planes and plow planes from this area are of this wood, as are hand adze handles. It is very similar to our live oak, except it is lighter brown and doesn't sink.

OAK, English

Also called brown oak, (because of its brown color, naturally). It sometimes has a striped or figured look.

OAK, Japanese

Lighter in color than our live oak, with straight grain and shorter, thinner rays. It is used in Japanese and Chinese planes.

WALNUT, Black

Except for some infills of English planes, a few measuring and homemade tools, not many tools are made of this wood. It is straight grained and brown in color, without any reddish cast. Although color is the best means of separating walnut from mahogany, end grain under 5X will help. It has more pores than mahogany, mainly due to walnut's pores diminishing in size as they move outward from the annual ring. This produces the telltale "shaded" look to the grain line in the flat section. Walnut's rays are very hard to see.

MAHOGANY, Central American (various species)

Commonly called Honduras Mahogany, from the former principal source, these look-alikes are light reddish brown with well defined pores in all sections. A ribboned appearance is common in mahogany, caused by changes in grain direction in adjacent areas. These woods are not as heavy as Cuban mahogany or the rosewoods, nor do they have the swirling dark stripes of the latter. Rays in the cross section are obvious under 5X, in contrast to walnut and rosewood. Mahogany is used in levels, measuring tools, and English plane infills.

MAHOGANY, Cuban

This wood is no longer available, but can be found in antique levels. It is considerably heavier than the Central American mahoganies, (bordering on sinking), and is tighter grained and much darker.

ROSEWOOD, East Indian (also called Indian Rosewood)

One of the premier tool woods. It has a medium brown to purplish brown color with dark brown (almost black) stripes. Pores can easily be seen in all sections under 5X, but not rays. It was used for plane handles, levels, measuring tools, premier planes, and braces.

ROSEWOOD, Brazilian

This more dramatically grained rosewood is dark brown to medium brown with swirling jet black stripes. It was used in similar ways to Indian rosewood. The difference between Brazilian and Indian is subtle when color is not a strong enough clue. Brazilian is heavier, more aromatic when abraded, and has tighter grain, (sparser pores). Unfortunately these three characteristics are not easy to evaluate in the finished tool. If you can't get a good look at the end grain, you may have to accept the fact that you can only identify it as a rosewood, nothing more. (Cocobolo is another species of rosewood that is very difficult to differentiate from Brazilian rosewood.)

ROSEWOOD, Honduras

A much lighter pinkish-brown to orangey-brown color with less figure and straighter grain than the rosewoods above. Used in premier planes and levels. It is generally heavy enough to sink.

LIGNUM VITAE

Common in Sheffield brace heads, it was also used in ship's planes, mallets, and in the boxing strips of planes from the Philadelphia area. The color varies (many times in the same piece) from olive brown to reddish brown with yellowish brown stripes. It generally becomes very dark with age. Its yellowish-tan sapwood may form part of a brace or plane, etc. The grain is very tight, and is distinctly interlocked (reversing). Pores can just about be seen at 5X, but not rays. A dusty (some say spicy) odor can be detected, even without scuffing. It sinks like a rock.

EBONY, Ceylon (now called Sri Lanka)

This basically black ebony has a light gray sapwood. It was used for braces (Ultimatums), plow planes, bow drills, ship's planes, infills for English planes, handles, and measuring tools. The pores are harder to pick out than the rosewoods; the rays are almost undetectable, even under 5X. Ceylon is the heaviest of the ebonys; it sinks quickly.

EBONY, Macassar

A dark brown ebony with medium brown stripes, and a buff colored sapwood. It was used in similar ways to Ceylon. Although not as dense as Ceylon, it still sinks.

EBONY, African (various species)

Some species have black heartwood, others a black and brown-striped heartwood, still others black with grayish-brown streaks. All have light colored sapwood, and all sink. Ebony is another group of species that might be hard to differentiate. Unfortunately, wood can vary drastically (even within a species), based upon growing conditions and locale. To get down to the nitty-gritty of which solid-black ebony is which, you will need more buzzwords, higher magnification, and lots of practice with known species samples.

The best way to learn these tool woods is to examine samples large enough to see all three sections. Some may be available from commercial sources, but some are no longer found, except in old tools.

BUYING ANTIQUE TOOLS

GARAGE and HOME SALES

Garage sale buying takes preparation. You should look carefully in the garage sale section of your newspaper for any indications of tools being included in the sale. However, just tools are not good enough; the ad must reflect "old" or "antique" tools. Even then, most of these sales will have only rusty wrenches, drills, and hammers that are not very old. Perhaps one time in ten, your perserverance will pay off with a real gem or two, often at very reasonable prices. Remember, the good stuff is usually gone in the first hour or so (sometimes the night before), so you're going to have to hustle. You have to like garage-saling, because most often it is not very productive.

FLEA MARKETS

These can be quite exciting, rather like a treasure hunt or like going fishing: getting up before dawn, having breakfast at the diner, and then hurrying off to try to haul in the "big one." The key here is to get to the "fishing hole" before anyone else does. And that ain't easy. Many others know which dealers have tools. You'll find a lot of familiar faces hovering around the same dealer, waiting for him to unload his station wagon. Of course, you can go on "upstream" to look for a new hole, and you might just get lucky. But you have to be quick and aggressive at times, and not too fussy about the weather.

At the big flea markets (such as Brimfield, MA; Bouckville, NY; Adamstown, PA) you'll almost always get something. Most of the experienced regulars "fly" through on their first pass, picking up obvious bargains, and then settle down to more detailed inspection on a second pass. Some avoid the rush and deliberately start later to catch dealers who are slower at setting up. A few will pay an early entrance fee that, at some markets, allows them to get in along with the dealers, before the general public. Whatever technique you use, it's almost always a fun day afield.

TOOL DEALERS

This is by far the most comfortable and most efficient way to buy. However, you should expect to pay the market price. Some shops are pricier than others, but even the high-priced shops have a bargain or two. In any event, these shops will usually have some fine tools to look at. It's a wonderful way to educate yourself while feasting your eyes.

Almost all dealers will bargain to some degree. But dealers have to make a living, and when you've hit their bottom line, you risk insulting them if you continue to haggle. If the price is still too high for you after the dealer has brought it down to his "best price," thank him and walk away. You want him as a friend.

Many tool dealers are in "co-op" type shops. Tool club newsletters will tell you where they are.

Some dealers publish tool catalogs. Most all contain photos and informative descriptions of several hundred tools for sale. To find out who is currently active, check tool club periodicals. The EAIA Directory (available to members of the Early American Industries Association - see Clubs and Organizations) lists 370 U.S. dealers in 46 states, and 17 in foreign countries.

ANTIQUE SHOWS

These often include tool dealers as well as general dealers who carry tools along with other items. Again, it's a good place to learn. The dealers are generally knowledgeable and friendly. Don't expect bargains, but unusual items do show up. Watch your newspapers for time and place.

TOOL AUCTIONS

Ah–the auction! Nothing equals it for drama, excitement, and pure entertainment. The five or six hundred lots at an auction assures you that there will be something for everyone. Auctions will give you a sense of market prices and will expose you to other collectors and dealers. The auction catalog, and the subsequent "Prices Realized" list, will provide you with a valuable reference.

You might feel somewhat intimidated in the beginning and hesitant to bid; most everyone does. That feeling will disappear after you've had a chance to participate. Most tool auctions are "country style" and the atmosphere is friendly and informal. Naturally, it's better to attend your first auction with a knowledgeable auction-goer. He can fill you in on the procedures, the other participants, and the by-play, and will soon have you bidding like a pro. But go, even if you have to go alone.

It's easy to be carried away at an auction, particularly if you're a competitive type. Two things to keep in mind:

1. Look carefully at each piece you plan to bid on during the preview before the auction. *It's best not to bid on any item you haven't inspected.*

2. Fix in your mind (on paper is even better) what you are willing to pay for an item and stick to it. You may miss a few bargains, but you'll avoid a lot of mistakes.

Below is a list of auctioneers who conduct periodic antique tool sales. Write and ask to be put on their mailing lists. There is usually a charge for auction catalogs. Some allow mail bids.

- Brown Auction Services: 27 Fickett Rd., Pownal, ME 04069.

- Fine Tool Journal: 27 Fickett Rd., Pownal, ME 04069.

- Barry Hurchalla: 249 Creek Rd., Boyertown, PA 19512.

- Live Free or Die: P.O. Box 281, Bath, NY 14810

- David Stanley Auction: Stordon Grange, Osgathorpe, Leicestershire, LE12 9SR, U.K.

- Bill Spicer: 276 Widow Sweets Rd., Exeter, RI 02822

- The Tool Shop Auction: The Tool Shop, 78 High St., Needham Market, Suffolk IPS 8AW, England.

- Tom Witte's Antiques: Front St. West, P.O. Box 399, Mattawan, MI 49071.

And now for the latest in technology relating to tool auctions: the **INTERNET AUCTION**. There are a number of such auctions, but the most significant one is eBay, which can be found under www.ebay.com. For the first time, people from the far-off parts of the earch can see and bid on antique tools (and almost anything else you can think of) via the computer. Actually, you don't even need a computer to do it, as you can buy a "black box" to attach to your TV that will allow you to do many things that a computer can do, including bidding on the Internet auctions. One such "box" is called WebTV, and is sold in almost all electronics stores. It is inexpensive and easy to use.

Whether you use a computer, or WebTV, the procedure is almost identical. Bring up eBay on your screen, select your category, and scroll down to the various individual items that are being auctioned. The category most used by antique tool sellers is COLLECTIBLES:TOOLS:WOODWORKING. There are other categories, and you will find some "sleepers" in some of the less descriptive categories. Once you get the hang of it, you can go directly to specific types of tools, and even to specific sellers.

All of these auctions have a time limit, 7 days in most cases. The auctions are timed so that they finish on the exact second. If you are as much as one second late, your bid will not count! There are a number of techniques that bidders use. Some bid right away, and they keep track of their bids that way. Others don't want anyone to know they are bidding, in order to prevent less knowledgeable bidders from "following" their action. They bid near the end.

The pièce de résistance of electronic bidding is called "sniping." It is acceptable, even though a lot of bidders grumble about it. It's done by waiting until the last few seconds of the auction (based on how fast your computer reacts) and then punching in your bid, not leaving time for anyone else to do likewise. Some people use two computers to do it; others have software designed to accomplish the same thing. But there are times when the electronics become overloaded and the sniper can't get the bid in before the auction ends. It's a bit of a crap-shoot.

A way to counteract the snipe is called a "proxy bid." With it, you specify the highest amount you are willing to bid. The nice part is that the "computer-in-the-sky" will keep your bid "in its pocket" and only raise the competing high bid by one bidding interval (just as in a live auction). It will go all the way to your limit *only* when needed to maintain your high bid status. In that way you keep your top bid secret for a while and might thwart a sniper.

A seller is allowed to post a "reserve" – the minimum he will accept for his tool. He has to announce that there *is* a reserve, but he need not disclose its dollar amount. Once the bid goes over the reserve, it is so stated on the screen and he is obligated to sell the tool to the highest bidder. There are refinements, such as late additions, cancellations, appeals, etc., but you can learn the nitty-gritty from experience.

The main thing to determine when bidding is WHO IS THE SELLER. Is he well known, reputable, knowledgeable? Does he claim to know what he is talking about, or does he merely say he knows nothing, and disclaims all responsibility for descriptive accuracy? How are the photos? Do they show all views, or is there a defect that might be hidden in a view not shown? You can E-mail the seller with your questions, but he may not answer in time, or he may again disclaim any knowledge.

There is a record kept on eBay of the responses to the seller's previous auctions from his buyers. It is called FEEDBACK and can give you some helpful information about your seller. On the other hand, some buyers may hesitate to say anything bad about a seller. So, although the Feedback chart is very helpful, don't fall in love with it.

The seller doesn't ship until the buyer's check is cashed or his money order is received. In almost all cases, a tool dealer who has been around a while (and you can tell that from a number that comes after his code name) will accept a tool back and return your money for almost any legitimate reason. If you feel squeamish about sending money to a stranger before receiving your merchandise, use the escrow system available from eBay.

In summary, buying tools from Internet auctions can be a very nice hobby for many who can't get to the live tool auctions, or live in areas that don't have many antique tools. It certainly has grown to enormous proportions in the past few years . . . Welcome aboard!

TABLE SALES and TAILGATE SALES

These are the best places to find up to 100 antique tool dealers displaying their finest merchandise for sale. Most national tool auctions feature these sales in conjunction with the auction. They are also held as tailgate sales before tool club meetings. These events are announced in the press, tool club periodicals, and in the flyers sent out by the auction houses.

CLUBS

The best way to get into the swing of "tooling" is to join a local tool club and also one of the national tool societies. (See Clubs and Organizations, page 136). Even if you are not a joiner, a club's publication is worth the minimal annual dues. You'll also get valuable information from the meeting programs and from your fellow members. And you'll be able to swap, buy, (and sell, if you wish) at each meeting.

CLUBS and ORGANIZATIONS

NATIONAL ORGANIZATIONS

EARLY AMERICAN INDUSTRIES ASSOCIATION (EAIA)

The oldest (founded in 1933) of the antique tool societies, it is international in scope. Members receive *The Chronicle,* a quarterly magazine on subjects relating to tools and collecting, and *Shavings*, a bi-monthly newsletter that lists meetings and events of interest to collectors. The Association offers members discounts on relevant books and the use of its library. Annual meetings are held around the country, often at well-known restorations, providing exhibits, lectures, seminars, tools sales and exchanges. Write Elton Hall, 167 Bakerville Rd., S. Dartmouth, MA 02748.

MID-WEST TOOL COLLECTORS ASSOCIATION (M-WTCA

A very active group. Despite its name, it is national in scope. There are two meetings a year, at which there is much tool buying and selling and swapping, as well as exhibits and educational programs. This group frequently underwrites and distributes reprints of old tool catalogs and other interesting material. The M-WTCA has a number of affiliated regional clubs that also conduct meetings and swaps. Write David E. Heckel, 1800 McComb, Charleston, IL 61920.

TOOL GROUP OF CANADA

A well organized and active group that, as the name implies, specializes in Canadian tools and early agricultural, maritime, and industrial development. Write Dan Wentworth, 153 Butter Rd. West, Ancaster, ONT L9G 3LI, Canada.

THE TOOLS AND TRADES HISTORY SOCIETY (TATHS)

This is the English tool society. It holds two meetings a year in such areas of interest as the Portsmouth Naval Yard and Iron Bridge. It publishes an excellent yearly journal and quarterly newsletter. Write to: The Administrator, 60 Swanley Lane, Swanley, Kent BR8 7JG, U.K.

HAND TOOL PRESERVATION ASSOCIATION of AUSTRALIA

Write Frank J. Ham, 21 Adeney Ave., KEW 3101, Victoria, Australia.

TRADES & TOOLS - NETHERLANDS

Write Gerrit van der Sterre, Acacialaan 18, 235 1 CC Leiderdorp, Netherlands.

REGIONAL and SPECIALIZED GROUPS

ANTIQUE TOOLS & TRADES IN CONNECTICUT (ATTIC)
Craig Jensen, PO Box 8196, Manchester, CT 06040.

COLLECTORS OF RARE AND FAMILIAR TOOLS SOCIETY OF NEW JERSEY (CRAFTS)
Joe Hauck, 85 Brunswick Ave., Lebanon, NJ 08833.

EARLY TRADES AND CRAFTS SOCIETY (LONG ISLAND, NY)
Sue Eckers, 11 Blythe Place, East Northport, NY 11731-3219.

LONG ISLAND TOOL COLLECTORS ASSOCIATION (LITCA)
Bill Hermanek, 31 Wildwood Lane, Smithtown, NY 11787.

NEW ENGLAND TOOL COLLECTORS ASSOCIATION (NETCA)
Ted Hopkins, RR2 Box 3265, Manchester Center, VT 05255.

OHIO TOOL COLLECTORS ASSOCIATION (OTCA),
John Walter, PO Box 227, Marietta, OH 45750.

PACIFIC NORTHWEST TOOL COLLECTORS (PNTC)
Jim Sebring, 19421 N.E. 162 St., Woodinville, WA 98072.

POTOMAC ANTIQUE TOOLS & INDUSTRIES ASSOCIATION (PATINA)
Sam Pickens, 3316 Circle Hill Rd., Alexandria, VA 22305.

PRESERVING ARTS & SKILLS OF THE TRADES ASSOCIATION (PAST)
Steve Habitz, 2243 Radnor Ave., Long Beach, CA 90815-2128.

ROCKY MOUNTAIN TOOL COLLECTORS (RMTC)
Steve Scruggs, 342 Sherman St., Longmont, CO 80501.

SOUTHWEST TOOL COLLECTORS ASSOCIATION (SWTCA)
Don Rosebrook, 38352 Henry Rd., Prairieville, LA 70769.

SOCIETY OF WORKERS IN EARLY ARTS AND TRADES (SWEAT)
Don Carpentier, Box 143, RD, East Nassau, NY 12062.

THREE RIVERS TOOL COLLECTORS (WESTERN PA.)
Bob Kendra, 3 10 Old Airport Rd., Greensburg, PA 15601.

WESTERN NEW YORK ANTIQUE TOOL COLLECTORS ASSN.
Frank Kosmerl, 432 Hollybrook Road, Rochester, NY 14623.

MISSOURI VALLEY WRENCH CLUB
Virgil Saak, Rt. 1, Box 53, Baxter, IA 50028

BIBLIOGRAPHY

Astragal Press publishes and distributes books on early tools, trades, and technology. A free booklist is available on request from Astragal Press, P.O. Box 239, Mendham, NJ 07945-0239.

AMERICAN LEVELS AND THEIR MAKERS, Vol. I, *Don Rosebrook.* The book covers over 80 companies and individuals that made and/or sold levels in New England (including Stanley, Davis, Stratton, Watts and Harmon), with a full discussion of each maker's product line and hundreds of photographs of sample levels. Where possible, there is an indication of the level's rarity. From Astragal Press.

AMERICAN LEVEL PATENTS ILLUSTRATED AND EXPLAINED, Vol. I, *Don Rosebrook.* Over 200 patents are pictured and explained, with explanations keyed to the patent drawings. Each patent is triply indexed. by date, patentee and category. From Astragal Press.

AMERICAN MACHINIST'S TOOLS: An Illustrated Directory of Patents, *Kenneth L. Cope.* The book illustrates and lists over 1000 fully indexed patents, covering all American machinist's tools patented through 1905, and the more important ones patented between 1906 and 1916. From Astragal Press.

AMERICAN MARKING GAGES – PATENTED AND MANUFACTURED, *Milton Bacheller.* Contains historical and product information on hundreds of known makers, as well as information on more than 350 marking gage patents. Available from the author, 185 South Street, Plainville, MA 02762

THE AMERICAN PATENTED BRACE 1829-1924: An Illustrated Directory of Patents, *Ronald W. Pearson.* Over 500 brace patents listed in three ways: alphabetically by patentee name, chronologically by date and patent number, and by type of brace. From Astragal Press.

AMERICAN WRENCH MAKERS, *Kenneth Cope.* Hundreds of makers are included, with each listing showing the maker information and known products. There is also a wrench identification section that cross-references patent dates and trade names to the actual maker. From Astragal Press.

ANTIQUE AND COLLECTIBLE STANLEY TOOLS, Guide to Identity and Value, Second Edition, *John Walter.* The classic collector's guide to Stanley tools and prices. It covers over 2100 individual tools, plus hundreds of additional listings for each significant type and model variation. Available from Astragal Press.

ANTIQUE & UNUSUAL WRENCHES, *Alfred & Lucille Schulz.* A profusely illustrated study of wrenches, including many rare varieties. Available from the authors, Rt.1, Box 151, Malcolm, NE 68402.

THE AXE AND MAN, *Charles Heavrin,* Covers the enormous range of axes used throughout time and the world, giving detailed descriptions of the axes, how they were made and used, and the evolution of their design over time. More than 100 photos accompany the descriptions, many of axes found only in museums. From Astragal Press.

AXE MAKERS OF NORTH AMERICA, *Allan Klenman.* An account of major manufacturers of axes in the U.S. and Canada, with material to help in the identification of axes. Available from Whistle Punk Books, 407-3260 Quadra Street, Victoria, B.C., Canada VOX lG2.

BOXWOOD & IVORY: Stanley Traditional Rules 1855-1975, *Philip E. Stanley.* This book lists, illustrates and explains all the different rules that Stanley ever made, from 1855 to 1975. The author traces the development of rule making, how rules were made, the materials that were used, and finally, how the various types of rules worked. Profusely illustrated. Available from the author, 36 Stockton St. #2, Worcester, MA 01610-2141.

BRITISH PLANEMAKERS FROM 1700, *W. L. Goodman.* Third edition. The recognized reference work on British planemakers. The biographic directory covers 1650 makers and dealers, and there are over 1600 imprint illustrations. From Astragal Press.

COLLECTING ANTIQUE TOOLS, *Herbert P. Kean and Emil S. Pollak.* The book describes and illustrates over 700 of the most important tools that are available to collectors. There are over 250 original photographs, plus many line drawings that show these tools in use. Also covered are valuable tips on cleaning, restoring, and displaying, as well as common and not so common pitfalls to avoid. From Astragal Press.

A DICTIONARY OF LEATHERWORKING TOOLS, *R.A. Salaman.* Describes and illustrates every tool used in the leatherworking trades from about 1700 to the present time. One of the author's classic works. From Astragal Press.

A DICTIONARY OF WOODWORKING TOOLS, *R.A. Salaman.* Revised edition, 1989. More an encyclopedia than a dictionary. With the help of detailed drawings, it explains the origin of virtually every woodworking hand tool, its purpose, its use, and (where known) who designed and made it. From Astragal Press.

HENRY DISSTON & SONS HANDBOOK FOR LUMBERMEN. This book describes and illustrates the Disston saws in great detail and explains how they were used, maintained, and installed. From Astragal Press.

GRIMSHAW ON SAWS. Written in 1880 by *Robert Grimshaw*, a founder of the American Society of Mechanical Engineers, it remains the definitive work describing and illustrating all types of saws from handsaws to the most advanced late 19th century models. Loaded with practical information on rake, saw setting, filing, and swaging. From Astragal Press.

A GUIDE TO THE MAKERS OF AMERICAN WOODEN PLANES Third Edition, *E.& M. Pollak.* This is the standard reference, a complete guide to all known American planemakers. Almost 2000 biographical entries, 2200 illustrated makers' marks, and 930 wedge outlines, along with sections on the various types of planes, a short history of planemaking in America, a glossary and a bibliography. From Astragal Press.

THE HAMMER: The King of Tools, *Ron Baird and Dan Comerford.* Provides hundreds of illustrations and information on approximately 200 American hammer patents. Available from Dan Comerford, Box 271, Stony Brook, NY 11790.

MAKERS OF AMERICAN MACHINIST'S TOOLS, *Kenneth L. Cope.* The first historical guide to describe both the makers and the tools they produced. Included are the major manufacturers such as Brown & Sharpe, L.S. Starrett, Standard Tool, Sawyer, and Stevens, as well as the many smaller firms who were often the innovators - altogether over 330 companies. With this there is background on the tools themselves, with very many illustrations. From Astragal Press.

MORE MAKERS OF AMERICAN MACHINIST'S TOOLS, *Kenneth L. Cope.* Covers hundreds of additional makers, and more material on the "Big Five" makers, with several of their previously unknown tools. Again, fully illustrated and researched. From Astragal Press.

MY FIRST 1000 WRENCHES, *Donald H. Snyder.* Illustrated and arranged by category. Available from the author, 12925 Woodworth Road, New Springfield, OH 94443.

PATENTED TRANSITIONAL & METALLIC PLANES IN AMERICA 1827-1927, Vol. 1, *Roger K. Smith.* The standard reference on American patented and metallic planes. Over 110 line drawings and 350 photographs, 41 in full color. Available from Roger K. Smith at P.O. Box 177, Athol, MA 01331.

PATENTED TRANSITIONAL & METALLIC PLANES IN AMERICA, Vol. II, *Roger K. Smith.* Continues where Vol. I left off. Over 450 photographs, 44 in full color, 300 line illustrations. Available from Roger K. Smith, P.O. Box 177, Athol, MA 01331.

PLANEMAKERS OF WESTERN PENNSYLVANIA, *Charles Prine, Jr.* A wonderful mixture of history, human interest and product description, this thoroughly researched book provides new insights into the lives of early 19th century planemakers in Pittsburgh and the surrounding areas, including Baltimore and Cincinnati. Superb photography. From Astragal Press.

BIBLIOGRAPHY

RESTORING ANTIQUE TOOLS, *Herbert P. Kean*. Explains restoration techniques that experts have long used. There are chapters on each of the major tool categories, as well as a general chapter on cleaning and refinishing. From Astragal Press.

SARGENT PLANES, Identification and Value Guide, *David E. Heckel*. A listing of Sargent's planes with their descriptions, illustrations, and value ranges. Also includes Sargent's history, trademarks, catalogs, and brand names. Available from the author, 1800 McComb St., Charleston, IL 61920.

THE SPOKE SHAVE BOOK: Manufactured and Patented Spoke Shaves and Similar Tools, *Thomas C. Lamond*. Profiles of the patentees and other makers, hundreds of diagrams and ads. Over 1000 artifacts pictured. Available from the author, 30 Kelsey Place, Lynbrook, NY 11563.

THE STANLEY COMBINATION PLANE. Invaluable for anyone who owns or uses a Stanley 45 or 55 combination plane. This special compilation covers the development of all major types of Stanley combination planes: the Miller's, the Traut's, as well as the Stanley 45 and 55. Their evolution is described and fully illustrated, the patent information and, in the case of the 45 and 55, copies of the original instructions, are included. From Astragal Press.

THROUGH MUCH TRIBULATION: Stewart Spiers and the Planemakers of Ayr, *Nigel Lampert*. A definitive study of the first major manufacturer of infill planes, describing and illustrating the historical, social and economic context in which the maker operated for over 100 years. From Astragal Press.

TOOLS: A Guide for Collectors, *Jane & Mark Rees*. Descriptions, illustrations, and interesting information on 80 categories of English tools. Many enjoyable collecting tips. 241 pages. From Astragal Press.

THE TOOLSHED TREASURY: The Best Articles on Antique Tool Collecting from CRAFTS. A wonderfully readable book of articles and stories taken from "The Tool Shed," the periodical published by the Collectors of Rare and Familiar Tools Society. Everyone involved with old tools will find something of interest here. From Astragal Press.

THE ULTIMATE BRACE, *Reg Eaton*. A beautifully illustrated and carefully researched study of the Sheffield metallic framed brace, providing an insight into Victorian trade practices. From Erica Jane Publishing, 35 High St., Heacham, Kings Lynn, Norfolk, England PE3 1 7DB.

THE WOODEN PLANE: Its History, Form & Function, *John M. Whelan*. Describes, illustrates, and classifies all types of wooden planes, from the common to the rare and unusual. As well as American and British planes, there are also French, Dutch, German, Japanese, and Chinese. A valuable and extraordinary book. From Astragal Press.

REPRINTS OF TOOL CATALOGS and TOOL CATALOG
COLLECTIONS (All available from Astragal Press)

A BROWN & SHARPE CATALOGUE COLLECTION, 1868 to 1899. Includes the company's 1868, 1887, and 1899 catalogs.

BUCK BROS. 1890 CATALOG. Buck, founded by immigrants from Sheffield, England, became world-renowned for its chisels: firmer, paring, carving, millwrights, framing, corner, and just about any other type.

H. CHAPIN 1859 PRICE LIST. One of the earliest price lists for a major planemaker.

CHAPIN-STEPHENS 1914 CATALOG. From one of the largest 19th century manufacturers of wooden planes, rules, and other hand tools, descriptions, illustrations, and prices of its complete line.

GREENFIELD TOOL CO. 1872 ILLUSTRATED CATALOG. The company's complete line, featuring many planes.

THE HANDSAW CATALOG COLLECTION. The handsaw section from a major early 20th century catalog of Henry Disston & Sons, Philadelphia, PA; Simonds Manufacturing Co. of Fitchburg, MA; and Spear & Jackson of Sheffield, England.

MILLERS FALLS COMPANY 1887 CATALOG. For 75 years Millers Falls was a leading tool manufacturer, particularly noted for its hand and breast drills. This fully illustrated early catalog contains these drills and many other items as diverse as boring machines, levels, saws, treadle lathes, and mitreboxes.

PECK, STOW & WILCOX COMPANY'S 1800 CENTENNIAL CATALOG: Tinsmith's Tools and Machines. Every imaginable piece of tinsmith's equipment from formers and stakes to double seamers, folding and wiring machines are listed, described, and illustrated.

THE PRESTON 1909 CATALOGUE. The 1909 catalogue lists and illustrates over 600 different rules, 300 levels, the distinctive Preston planes, and a variety of other tools and instruments. This is one of the most attractive of all the English tool trade catalogues. 224 pages. Hundreds of illustrations.

THE RUSSELL JENNINGS MFG. CO. 1899 CATALOG. Russell Jennings was synonymous with drill bits and the 1899 catalog shows why, with its beautifully illustrated and fully described presentation.

SANDUSKY TOOL CO. 1877 CATALOG. This catalog includes the boxwood, rosewood and ebony classic centerwheel plows and the Morris Patent, among others.

SANDUSKY TOOL CO. 1925 CATALOG. The last catalog issued by this important wooden plane manufacturer, containing its complete line, including weatherstrip planes, coopers' tools, and other interesting items. Many illustrations and molding profiles.

THE SARGENT TOOL CATALOG COLLECTION. Contains all the Sargent tools that were listed and illustrated in three of its major catalogs, the 1894, 1910, and 1922. There is a full range of woodworking tools.

THE STANLEY CATALOG COLLECTION. An important reference that contains complete reprints of seven of the most significant 19th century Stanley catalogs, the 1855, 1859, 1867, 1870-71, 1879, 1888, and 1898. Fully indexed. Hundreds of illustrations.

THE STANLEY CATALOG COLLECTION, VOL. II. Included are catalog reprints from 1872, 1874 (revised to 1876), 1877, 1884, and 1892 (revised to 1897), in addition to the Leonard Bailey catalogs of 1876 and 1883.

INDEX

NOTES